real life

elementary

WORKBOOK

contents

starter 1

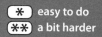
Vocabulary

Countries and nationalities

1 Rearrange the letters to make countries.

1 zrabli   _Brazil_
2 eht ku   _____
3 niagenrta   _____
4 het sau   _____
5 kutery   _____

2 Write the nationality of each country in the correct column.

> Ireland   Brazil ✓   The UK   Hungary
> Scotland   Spain   Argentina   Mexico
> Poland   Italy   The USA   Turkey

-ian	-an	-ish
Brazilian		

3 Complete the gaps with the correct country or nationality.

1 Paella is a _Spanish_ dish.
2 Dublin is in _____ .
3 Madonna is an _____ singer.
4 Istanbul is a city in _____ .
5 Pizza is _____ .
6 Edinburgh is the capital city of _____ .
7 Shakespeare is _____ .
8 Buenos Aires is the capital of _____ .

Grammar

Verb *to be* singular

4 ✱ Underline the correct form of the verb *to be*.

1 Peter *are/is* a student.
2 You *are not/am not* in my class.
3 I *isn't/'m not* a teacher.
4 *Is/Is not* Eve from Poland?
5 She *isn't/aren't* Turkish.
6 His name *am/is* Patrick.
7 *Is/Are* you from Prague?
8 I *am/are* in the football team.

5 ✱✱ Put the words in the correct order to make questions. Then write the short answer.

1 you/student/are/a? (✓)
  Are you a student? Yes, I am.
2 Spanish/is/she? (✗)
  _____
3 they/brother and sister/are? (✗)
  _____
4 friends/are/we? (✓)
  _____
5 is/from/Spain/he? (✓)
  _____
6 a/is/teacher/she? (✗)
  _____
7 class/in/you/are/my? (✗)
  _____
8 she/Scottish/is? (✓)
  _____

Subject pronouns and possessive adjectives

6 (✱✱) Complete the sentences with the words below.

> its his he she her I ✓
> my your

1 My name is James, _I_ am English.
2 She is in my class, _____ name is Sophie.
3 Sophie isn't Italian, _____ is Argentinian.
4 Are _____ friends Spanish?
5 Is this your dog? What's _____ name?
6 Alex is fourteen, it's _____ birthday today!
7 Is Alex in the football team? Yes, _____ is.
8 I'm Irish but _____ mother is Scottish.

7 (✱✱) Replace the underlined word with the correct subject pronoun or possessive adjective.

1 Tina and Fred aren't American.
  Tina and Fred are English.   _They_
2 Tina and Fred's parents
  are Brazilian.   _____
3 Are you and I in the
  basketball team?   _____
4 Toby isn't in the basketball team.
  Toby is in the football team.   _____
5 My dog is cute.
  My dog's name is Alf.   _____
6 Ayla is in my class. Ayla is Turkish. _____
7 Sarah is fifteen. Sarah's birthday
  is in April.   _____
8 You and I are Mexican.   _____

Verb *to be* plural

8 (✱) Complete the sentences with the correct form of the verb *to be*.

1 Nancy and I _are_ from Galway. (+)
2 You and Sam _____ in my class. (–)
3 Me and my brother _____ in the
  same class. (+)
4 The girls _____ in the basketball team. (–)
5 _____ our teachers English? (?)
6 Our parents _____ Spanish, they
  _____ Brazilian. (–/+)
7 The students _____ from Madrid. (+)
8 My friends _____ in the football team. (–)

Grammar reference

Verb *to be* singular

	Affirmative	Negative
I	*am ('m)* a teenager.	*am not ('m not)* a teenager.
You	*are ('re)* a teenager.	*are not (aren't)* a teenager.
He/She/It	*is ('s)* a teenager.	*is not (isn't)* a teenager.

Yes/No questions	Short answers
Am I a teenager?	Yes, I *am.* No, I'm not.
Are you a teenager?	Yes, you *are.* No, you *aren't.*
Is she/he/it a teenager?	Yes, he/she/it *is.* No, he/she/it *isn't.*

Wh- questions

What is your name?
Where is Chris from?

Verb *to be* plural

	Affirmative	Negative
We/You/They	*are ('re)* Spanish.	*are not (aren't)* Spanish.

Yes/No questions	Short answers
Are we/you/they Spanish?	Yes, we/you/they *are* Spanish. No, we/you/they *aren't* Spanish.

Wh- questions

Where are your parents from?

Subject pronouns and possessive adjectives

Subject pronouns	Possessive adjectives
I	my
you	your
he	his
she	her
it	its

Subject pronouns and possessive adjectives plural

Subject pronouns	Possessive adjectives
we	our
you	your
they	their

Our teacher is English.
Are *your* names Tom and Nick?
What is *their* favourite football team?

starter 2

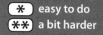

Vocabulary

School equipment

1 _bookshelf_
2 _____
3 _____
4 _____
5 _____
6 _____
7 _____
8 _____
9 _____

1 Look at the picture and label the objects.

2 Look at the picture again and <u>underline</u> the correct word.

1 The pencil is *on/<u>next to</u>* the pencil sharpener.
2 The calculator is *under/on* the pencil case.
3 The dictionary is *on/in* the bookshelf.
4 The bag is *near/next to* the desk.
5 The scissors are *in/on* the pencil case.
6 The pencil case is *on/under* the desk.

3 Look at the clocks and write the times.

1 It's _nine o'clock_ .

2 It's _____ .

3 It's _____ .

4 It's _____ .

5 It's _____ .

6 It's _____ .

4 Write the numbers in full.

1 1002   _one thousand and two_
2 54,900 _____
3 546   _____
4 78   _____
5 4,670   _____
6 90   _____
7 9,922   _____
8 32,600 _____
9 8,312   _____
10 234   _____

Grammar

Singular and plural nouns

5 (*) Put the words in the correct column.

pen ✓ ruler eraser computer box
dictionary exercise book orange
desk interactive whiteboard calculator

a	an
pen	

4

6 (*) Write the plural forms of the words.

1 book _____ books _____
2 box _____
3 orange _____
4 class _____
5 watch _____
6 computer _____

7 (**) Put the words in the correct order to make sentences.

1 my/is/this/book
_____ This is my book. _____

2 are/these/desks/your
_____

3 her/are/pencils/those?
_____

4 brother/he/is/their/not
_____

5 our/this/is/teacher
_____

6 his/dogs/these/are
_____

7 that/my/is/computer?
_____

8 not/are/our/those/pens
_____

8 (*) Complete the sentences with *these*, *that*, *this* or *those*.

1 Are _these_ your pens?

2 _____ is my dog.

3 Are _____ your books?

4 _____ isn't my dictionary.

Grammar reference

Singular and plural nouns

Singular nouns

We use *a* or *an* with singular nouns.

- *a* is used before nouns starting with a consonant sound,

a calculator, a dictionary, a pencil

- *an* is used before nouns starting with a vowel sound,

an exercise book, an eraser, an orange

Plural nouns

To make plural nouns, we add –*s* to a singular noun:
ruler → rulers, cupboard → cupboards, computer → computers

We add -*es* to singular nouns ending in *ch, sh, s, x* and *o*.
watch → watches, box → boxes, bus → buses

this, that, these, those

We use *this, that, these, those* when we point at something.

- We use *this* and *these* for things which are near to you,

→ □
this pen
This is my pen.

→ □□
these pens
These are my pens.

- We use *that* and *those* for things which are far from you,

──────► □
that pen
That's my pen.

──────► □□
those pens
Those are my pens.

- We use *this* and *that* with singular nouns,
this computer, this book, that student, that dictionary

- We use *these* and *those* with plural nouns,
these computers, these books, those students, those dictionaries

5

it's my life

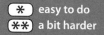
✳ easy to do
✳✳ a bit harder

Vocabulary

My things

1 Look at the pictures and complete the crossword.

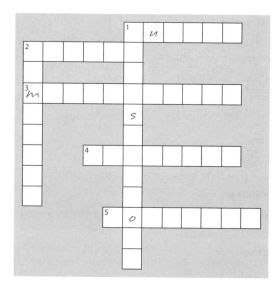

Across

1

2

3

4 (football image)

5

Down

1 (handheld game console image)

2

2 Tick (✓) the different word in each group.

1	phone	pet ✓	camera
2	friend	classmate	computer
3	skateboard	bicycle	goldfish
4	songs	computers	guitar
5	pet	goldfish	bicycle
6	band	bicycle	songs

Grammar

have got

3 ✳ What does 's mean in each sentence? <u>Underline</u> *is* or *has*.

Charlie's blog   Home   Fr

1	Lily's sixteen.	*is/has*
2	She's from Brighton.	*is/has*
3	She's got a brother.	*is/has*
4	She's music mad.	*is/has*
5	She's got 500 songs on her MP3 player.	*is/has*
6	She's got an electric guitar.	*is/has*

4 ✳✳ Put the words in the correct order to make sentences.

1 got/electric/she/guitar/an/has

   She has got an electric guitar.

2 a/TV/I/have/got

   _____.

3 Lily/phone/has/a/got/mobile

   _____.

4 goldfish/Paul/a/got/not/has

   _____.

5 not/they/a/got/computer/have

   _____.

6 DVD/got/player/a/they/have

   _____.

5 ✳✳ Write questions with *has got* or *have got*.

1 Lily/brother

   Has Lily got a brother?

2 Lily/pet

   _____

3 Peter/new bicycle

   _____

4 They/mobile phones

   _____

5 You/camera

   _____

6 He/computer

   _____

6 (*) **Read the questions and write the correct short answer.**

1 Has Maria got a brother? (✓)

   <u>Yes, she has.</u>

2 Has Peter got a pet? (✓)

   _____

3 Has Tony got an electric guitar? (✗)

   _____

4 Have your friends got cameras? (✓)

   _____

5 Have you got an MP3 player? (✗)

   _____

6 Has Paul got a nickname? (✗)

   _____

7 (**) **Complete the letter from Dima to Charlie with the words below.**

[I'm ✓   I've got   is (x2)   are   there are]

Hi Charlie,

I'm Dimitri Marcovitch. My nickname's Dima. ¹ <u>I'm</u> from St Petersburg. I've got two interests: football and music. I'm in the school football team. My favourite football team ² _____ Zenit FC in St Petersburg.

I'm music mad. ³ _____ an electric guitar and I'm in a band with my friends. My band is 'The Nevachiefs'. I've got one brother called Igor. He's in the band with me. Igor hasn't got an electric guitar. Igor ⁴ _____ the singer in the band. ⁵ _____ three bands in the school.

Where ⁶ _____ you from? Are you in a football team? Are you in a band? Have you got an electric guitar?

Bye!
Dima.

Grammar reference

have got

Form

+	I/You/We/They **have got ('ve got)** / He/She/It **has got ('s got)**	a house.
–	I/You/We/They **have not got (haven't got)** / He/She/It **has not got (hasn't got)**	
?	**Have** I/you/we/they **got** / **Has** he/she/it **got**	a house?

Short answers	Yes, I/you/we/they **have**. No, I/you/we/they **haven't**. Yes, he/she/it **has**. No, he/she/it **hasn't**.

Wh- questions	Answers
What has she got in her bag?	She's got a purse in her bag.
How many children have they got?	They've got two children.

Use

We use *have got* to talk about:

• possession

She**'s got** a dog.
We **haven't got** a computer.
Have you **got** a mobile phone?

• family members

I**'ve got** two cousins.
Tom **hasn't got** brothers or sisters.
Has she **got** a husband?

it's my life

7

Vocabulary

My family

1 Complete the words.

1 f _a_ _m_ i l y
2 m _ _ _ e r
3 f _ t h _ _
4 b _ _ _ _ _ r
5 g _ _ _ _ f _ _ _ e r
6 c h _ _ _ _ _ n

2 Choose words from exercise 1 to complete the sentences.

1 My _____ and _____ are my parents.
2 There are six people in my _____ .
3 My uncle and aunt have got two _____ .
4 I've got one sister and two _____s.
5 My _____ is ninety-four years old! He's great!

3 Look at the pictures. Complete the sentences with the words below.

> beard   moustache   glasses   fair   dark
> long ✓   short

Tina

Ted

Tim

1 Tina is twelve years old. She's got _long_ , _____ hair and _____ .
2 Tim has got a moustache but he hasn't got a _____ .
3 Tim has got _____ hair.
4 Ted has got short, _____ hair.
5 Ted has got a beard but he hasn't got a _____ .

Grammar

Possessive '*s*

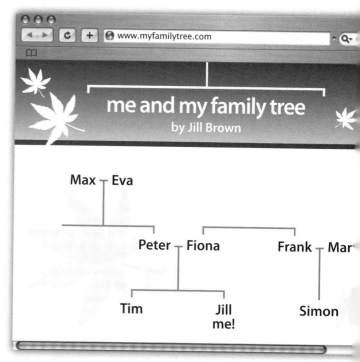

www.myfamilytree.com

me and my family tree
by Jill Brown

Max — Eva

Peter — Fiona   Frank — Mar

Tim   Jill
me!

Simon

4 (✱) Look at Jill's family tree. Complete the sentences with the correct name using possessive '*s*.

1 Peter is _Fiona's_ husband.
2 Marta is _____ wife.
3 Jill is _____ sister.
4 Frank is _____ brother.
5 Eva and Max are _____ and _____ grandparents.
6 Frank and Marta are _____ parents.
7 Simon is Tim and Jill's _____ .
8 Tim and Jill are Peter and Fiona's _____ .

5 (✱) Underline the correct words.

1 Hi! I'm Jill. I'm *Tims/Tim's/Tims'* sister.
2 My *fathers/father's/fathers'* name is Peter.
3 Our *parents/parent's/parents'* names are Fiona and Peter.
4 Eva is my *father's/fathers'/father* mother. She is my grandmother.
5 *Frank and Martas/Frank and Marta's/Frank and Martas'* son is Simon. He's my cousin.
6 Max and Eva are *my grandparents'/grandparent's/grandparents*.

Grammar Plus: 's

6 (✱✱) **Read the sentences. What does 's mean in each sentence? Underline is, has or possessive.**

1 Peter's moustache is dark.   *is/has/possessive*
2 Jill's got long, fair hair.   *is/has/possessive*
3 I've got a pet. It's a cat.   *is/has/possessive*
4 My cat's name is Blackie.   *is/has/possessive*
5 Frank's my uncle.   *is/has/possessive*
6 I am my parent's son.   *is/has/possessive*
7 She's my sister.   *is/has/possessive*
8 Tom's hair is brown.   *is/has/possessive*

7 (✱) **Look at the family tree in exercise 4 again. Write 's, s' or s.**

1 My father_'s_ name is Peter.
2 Peter and Fiona are my parent____ .
3 I am Peter and Fiona____ son.
4 Max and Eva are my grandparent____ .
5 Peter is my grandparent____ son.
6 Eva is my grandfather____ wife.
7 Jill is Tim____ brother.
8 Simon is Marta____ son.

8 (✱✱) **Answer the questions about the family tree in exercise 4.**

1 Who is Jill?
   She's Tim's sister.
2 Who is Fiona?
   _____ Peter____ wife.
3 Who is Simon?
   _____ Tim and Jill____ cousin.
4 Who is Marta?
   _____ Jill____ aunt.
5 Who are Max and Eva?
   _____ Peter____ parents.
6 Who are Tim and Jill?
   _____ Peter and Fiona____ children.
7 Who is Frank?
   _____ Marta____ husband.
8 Who is Max?
   _____ Tim and Jill____ grandfather.

Grammar reference

Possessive 's

Form

Singular nouns	my sister**'s** bag Kate**'s** boyfriend
Plural nouns regular	my brothers**'** names my paren**ts'** car
Plural nouns irregular	her children**'s** teacher people**'s** names

My father's name is David. (father = a singular noun)
Robert's camera is very good. (Robert = a singular noun)

My sisters' names are Imogen and Claire.
(sisters = regular plural noun)
My grandparents' garden is very big.
(grandparents = regular plural noun)

This is my children's school.
(children = irregular plural noun)
I don't know these women's names.
(women = irregular plural noun)

Notice!

My brother's name is Mark. (= I've got one brother)
My brothers' names are Tom and Ian.
(= I've got two brothers)

Use

We use the possessive 's to talk about people and their possessions.
Paul's dog is very big.
My best friends' names are Joanna and Georgia.
Is this Peter's book?

There are three different uses of 's in writing:

• to show possession.
This is Tom's bag.
I like your father's car.

• the short form of *is*.
She's from Spain. (she's = she is)
He's very nice. (he's = he is)
It's open. (it's = it is)

• the short form of *have got*.
He's got two brothers. (he's got = he has got)
She's got a dog. (she's got = she has got)
It's got 250 calories. (it's got = it has got)

Vocabulary

What's in your bag?

1 Look at the picture and label the objects with the words below.

> keys   lip salve ✓   packet of tissues
> purse   hairbrush   MP3 player

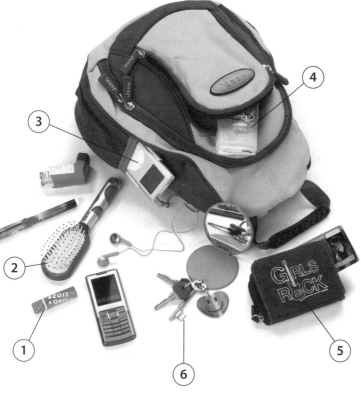

1 *lip salve*   4 _____
2 _____   5 _____
3 _____   6 _____

2 Complete the sentences with the words below.

> photos   mobile phone   keys ✓
> MP3 player   hairbrushes   chewing gum

1 I've got *keys* for my house and my moped.
2 My sister's got fifty-two contacts on her _____ .
3 Peter's got a lot of songs on his _____ .
4 I've got two _____ of my boyfriend.
5 Lily's got two _____ in her bag.
6 Karl's got a packet of _____ in his bag.

Grammar

there is/there are

3 ⊛ Complete the sentences with *There is* or *There are*.

1 *There is* a packet of tissues in my bag.
2 _____ a hairbrush in my room.
3 _____ two pencils on my desk.
4 _____ an inhaler in my bag.
5 _____ fifty-two songs on my MP3 player.
6 _____ two packets of chewing gum in my bag.

4 ⊛⊛ Put the words in the correct order to make questions. Then write short answers.

1 there/pen/in/is/bag/your/a/? (✓)
   Is there a pen in your bag?
   Yes, there is.

2 is/packet of tissues/there/your/bag/in/a/? (✗)
   _____
   _____

3 two/are/keys/bag/there/your/in/? (✓)
   _____
   _____

4 in/your/photo/wallet/is/a/there/? (✓)
   _____
   _____

5 two/are/bag/your/there/notebooks/in/? (✗)
   _____
   _____

6 purse/is/there/her/an ID card/in/? (✓)
   _____
   _____

7 hairbrush/there/is/a/your/in/bag/? (✗)
   _____
   _____

8 photos/are/there/desk?/on/the/? (✗)
   _____
   _____

Plural nouns

5 (✱✱) Complete the sentences describing the picture with the correct plural noun.

1 There are two <u>women</u> (woman) in the café.
2 There are three _____ (child) in the café.
3 There are two _____ (person) in the street.
4 There are two _____ (man) in the café.

Possessive pronouns

6 (✱) Match the pronouns in column A with the possessive pronouns in column B.

A   B
1 I   a hers
2 you   b ours
3 he   c theirs
4 she   d his
5 we   e mine
6 they   f yours

7 (✱) Underline the correct words.

1 I've got my keys. Have you got *you/your/yours*?
2 Tim's got his notebook but I haven't got *my/me/mine*.
3 I haven't got my brother's phone. My sister has got *him/his/he*.
4 Ben hasn't got Lily's dictionary. *She/Her/Hers* is on her desk.
5 This is the band's guitar. It's *theirs/they/their*.
6 Have you got your bags? We've got *our/us/ours*.

Grammar reference

there is/there are

Form

	Singular	Plural
+	**There is (There's)** a book.	**There are** two bicycles.
–	**There is not (isn't)** a book.	**There are not (aren't)** two bicycles.
?	**Is there** a book?	**Are there** two bicycles?
Short answers	Yes, **there is.** No, **there isn't.**	Yes, **there are.** No, **there aren't.**

Use

We use *there is/there are* + a noun to talk about where a thing or a person is or isn't.

There isn't a book on the table.
There are two mirrors in my room.
Are there ten boys in your class?

Possessive adjectives and pronouns

Possessive adjectives	Possessive pronouns
my book	mine
your book	yours
his book	his
her book	hers
its book	–
our book	ours
your book	yours
their book	theirs

When we talk about possession we can use possessive adjectives + a noun or possessive pronouns.

*This is **my computer**.* (possessive adjective *my* + a noun)
*It's **mine**.* (possessive pronoun *mine*)

*Is this **your wallet**?* (possessive adjective *your* + a noun)
*Is it **yours**?* (possessive adjective *yours*)

*It isn't **their car**.* (possessive adjective *their* + a noun)
*This car isn't **theirs**.* (possessive adjective *theirs*)

Writing

An email

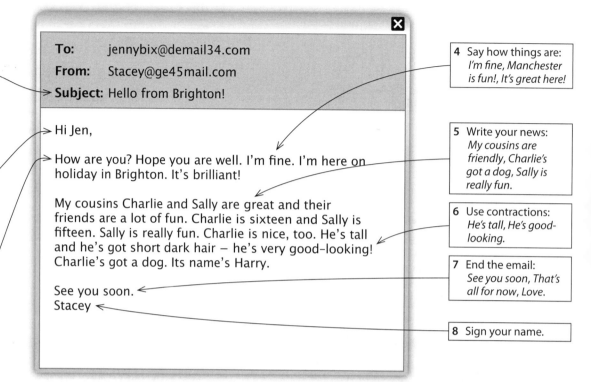

1 Give the email a title in the subject line: *Greetings from London, Hello from Brighton!*

2 Open the email with *Hi, Hello* or *Dear* + first name: *Dear Mum, Hello Mark, Hi Katy,* Don't forget the comma (,) after the name.

3 Ask how things are. Use an informal phrase: *How are you? I hope you're well.*

To: jennybix@demail34.com

From: Stacey@ge45mail.com

Subject: Hello from Brighton!

Hi Jen,

How are you? Hope you are well. I'm fine. I'm here on holiday in Brighton. It's brilliant!

My cousins Charlie and Sally are great and their friends are a lot of fun. Charlie is sixteen and Sally is fifteen. Sally is really fun. Charlie is nice, too. He's tall and he's got short dark hair – he's very good-looking! Charlie's got a dog. Its name's Harry.

See you soon.
Stacey

4 Say how things are: *I'm fine, Manchester is fun!, It's great here!*

5 Write your news: *My cousins are friendly, Charlie's got a dog, Sally is really fun.*

6 Use contractions: *He's tall, He's good-looking.*

7 End the email: *See you soon, That's all for now, Love.*

8 Sign your name.

---

1 Read the email and answer the questions.

1 Where is Stacey? _____

2 Who is Harry? _____

2 Complete Jenny's email with the phrases below.

> Dear   That's all for now.   How are you?   The school is fun!
> I'm fine.   My summer school ✓

To: Stace@grapple.com

From: jenny34@grapple.com

Subject: ¹ *My summer school*

² _____ Stacey,

³ _____ I hope you are well. ⁴ _____ I'm here in London.

The students are very friendly and the teachers are very nice.

My teacher's names are Mr Stevens and Mr Cliven.

⁵ _____

⁶ _____

Love,
Jenny

3 Put the phrases below into the correct column.

> that's all for now
> I hope you are well ✓
> How are you?   love
> Hi Jenny   Dear Mum
> Speak to you soon
> See you soon

Opening

1 *I hope you are well.*

2 _____

3 _____

4 _____

Closing

5 _____

6 _____

7 _____

8 _____

4 Change the underlined phrases to contracted forms.

To: mum@demail37.com
From: karen56@grapple.com
Subject: How are you?

Dear Mum and Dad,

How are you? ¹ I am fine. ² I am here in Brighton! ³ It is great.

⁴ Jane is great and her family is very friendly. Her parents are very nice and her sister Gill is fun. ⁵ She is fifteen. ⁶ She is tall and ⁷ she has got long hair.

⁸ That is all for now.

Love,
Karen

1 _I'm_
2 _____
3 _____
4 _____
5 _____
6 _____
7 _____
8 _____

5 Complete the strategies box with the words below.

dear + name   news   say   name
subject ✓

Writing an email

- Give the email a ¹ _subject_ .
- Open the email with *Hi*, or ² _____ .
- Ask how things are and also ³ _____ how things are.
- In the main paragraph write your ⁴ _____ .
- End your email and sign your ⁵ _____ .

6 Read the task and then write your email. Use the strategies in exercise 5 to help you.

Imagine you are on holiday with your cousins. Write an email to your friend.

- Say how you are.
- Ask how they are.
- Write your news.

Speaking

Meeting and greeting

7 Put the phrases in the correct order to make a dialogue.

a ☐ Pleased to meet you, too.
b ☑ This is Sam.
c ☐ Hi, Peter, pleased to meet you.
d ☐ Hi, Sam, I'm Peter.

Getting to know people

8 Match the questions 1–5 with the answers a–e.

1 Where are you from?
2 Have you got brothers or sisters?
3 How old are you?
4 Is this your first time in London?
5 What is your favourite music?

a Yes, it is.
b I haven't got a brother but I've got a sister.
c Rock.
d Barcelona.
e Sixteen.

9 Complete the dialogue with the phrases below.

it   Where   old   sisters   Pleased
your   I'm ✓   Hi   brothers   What

A: Hello. ¹ _I'm_ Jim
B: ² _____ Jim, I'm Katie.
A: ³ _____ to meet you, Katie. ⁴ _____ are you from?
B: I'm from Southampton, in England.
A: Have you got brothers or ⁵ _____ ?
B: I've got two ⁶ _____ . Their names are David and Michael.
A: How ⁷ _____ are they?
B: They are ten and fourteen.
A: Is this ⁸ _____ first time in Italy?
B: No, ⁹ _____ isn't. But it's my first time in Venice.
A: ¹⁰ _____ 's your favourite food?
B: Erm … pizza?

2 your day

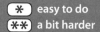
Vocabulary

School life

1 Look at the pictures and label the school subjects.

1 M _u s i c_

2 S c _ _ n c _

3 _ r t

4 P h y s _ c _ l E d _ c _ t _ _ n

2 Match the sentences 1–6 with the school subjects a–f.

1 'Go is an irregular verb.'   **a** Science
2 'Beethoven is a famous composer.'   **b** Music
3 'Cairo is a big city in Egypt.'   **c** Art
4 'Draw a picture of your classmate.'   **d** English
5 'There is no water on the moon.'   **e** Maths
6 'What is 354 + 235?'   **f** Geography

3 Complete the sentences with the words below.

> student ✓   teacher   class   lessons
> uniform   subject

1 I'm a _student_ at Latimer High School.
2 There are thirty-eight students in my _____ .
3 Mr Maddigan is my English _____ .
4 There are seven _____ every day.
5 My favourite _____ is PE.
6 I wear a school _____ . It's blue and white.

Grammar

Present simple affirmative

4 ** Read Marta's profile and complete the sentences.

> **PROFILE CARD**
>
> _My day_
>
> Get up: 7.00
> Go to school: by bus
> Start school: 8.30
> Lunch: in town with friends
> Finish school: 3.30
> After school: have saxophone lessons, do homework
> In the evening: watch TV
> Go to bed: 11.00
>
> Me – Marta

1 (get up) _Marta gets up at 7.00._
2 (go to school)
   _____
3 (start school)
   _____
4 (lunch)
   _____
5 (finish school)
   _____
6 (after school)
   _____
7 (in the evening)
   _____
8 (go to bed)
   _____

5 * Complete the sentences with the correct form of the verbs.

1 She always _carries_ (carry) her ID card.
2 Mr Simpson _____ (teach) geography.
3 Rosa _____ (watch) TV after school.
4 Kate _____ (do) her homework in the library.
5 Orlando _____ (go) to the sports club in the afternoon.
6 My English lesson _____ (finish) at 4.30.
7 Katrina _____ (tidy) her desk after school.
8 My aunt always _____ (wear) glasses.

Time expressions

6 (*) Write sentences about Dan's weekend. Use *always* (****), *usually* (***), *often* (**), *sometimes* (*) and *never*.

Dan's weekend

do sport in the evening   ****
listen to music   ***
go to parties   **
play the guitar   *
do homework on Saturdays

1 He _often_ goes to parties.
2 He _____ plays the guitar.
3 He _____ does sport in the evening.
4 He _____ listens to music.
5 He _____ does homework on Saturdays.

Grammar Plus: Position of time expressions

7 (**) Rewrite the sentences with the time expressions in the correct place.

1 My dad and I go to the football stadium on Saturdays. (usually)

   My dad and I usually go to the
   football stadium on Saturdays.

2 My sister wears sunglasses. (often)

   _____
   _____ .

3 I go to school on Saturdays. (never)

   _____
   _____ .

4 I tidy my room on Saturday morning. (always)

   _____
   _____ .

5 We have lunch in a restaurant. (once a week)

   _____
   _____ .

6 Jose and Julio watch MTV. They love music! (always)

   _____
   _____ !

Grammar reference

Present simple affirmative and time expressions

Form

+	I/You/We/They **play**	football.
	He/She/It **plays**	

Use

We use the present simple:

- to talk about habits/routines.

*I **get up** at seven o'clock every day.*
*She always **cycles** to school.*
*They **tidy** the classroom after their lessons.*

- to talk about facts/things that are generally true.

*Lessons **finish** at 3 p.m.*
*We **live** in Warsaw.*
*He **speaks** English and French.*

Spelling of third person forms in affirmative sentences

- When verbs end in a consonant + *y*, *-y* becomes *-ies.*

carry → carr**ies**, try → tr**ies**

- When verbs end in *-ch*, *-sh*, *-o*, we add *-es.*

watch → watch**es**, finish → finish**es**, go → go**es**

- An important exception is the third person singular of *have.*

have → has

Time expressions

To say <u>how often</u> we do things we can use adverbs of frequency.

100% ■■■■■■   0%
always   usually   often   sometimes   never

*Tom **always** does his homework in the evening.*
*My mother **usually** goes to work in the morning.*
*We **often** go to the library.*
*I **sometimes** have breakfast in bed.*
*They **never** go to school by bus.*

Position of time expressions

- We put adverbs *always, usually, often, sometimes, never* <u>before</u> most verbs.

*I **always** <u>take</u> a bus to work.   She **never** <u>drinks</u> milk.*

- We put adverbs *always, usually, often, sometimes, never* <u>after</u> the verb *to be.*

*Robert <u>is</u> **usually** here on time.   I <u>am</u> **sometimes** unhappy.*

- We put adverbs *always, usually, often, sometimes, never* <u>after</u> *not* in negative sentences.

*I <u>don't</u> **usually** eat chocolate.*
*She's <u>not</u> **often** hungry at school.*

- We put longer time expressions at the end of the sentence.

*We go to Spain **twice a year**.*
*Anna watches TV **in the evening**.*

your day

15

Vocabulary

Routine

1 Label the activities with the words below.

> wake up ✓   have a shower   go to bed
> go to school   watch TV   have breakfast

1 _wake up_   3 _____   5 _____
2 _____   4 _____   6 _____

2 Maria is an exchange student from Madrid. Read her letter to her friend Anna and complete the sentences with the words below.

> wake up ✓   have breakfast   get dressed
> walk to school   do homework
> watch TV   do sport   go home

Hi Anna,

I'm here in London – it's great! Here's what I do every day. Every morning I ¹ _wake up_ at half past seven. I ² _____ in the kitchen with Natalie – she's sixteen, too. Then I ³ _____ . Natalie and I ⁴ _____ at half past eight. Natalie's friend Kate walks with us. After school, we usually go to Kate's house. We ⁵ _____ together (I help them with Spanish!) and then we often ⁶ _____ (there are some good programmes in England). Sometimes we ⁷ _____ in the park near Kate's house – there are tennis courts there. We usually ⁸ _____ at seven o'clock.

Write soon!
Maria

Grammar

Present simple negative

3 (＊) Complete the sentences with *don't* or *doesn't*.

1 Georgia _doesn't_ eat hamburgers. She likes salads.
2 David _____ live in Verona. He lives in Venice.
3 My parents _____ play computer games very often.
4 Chris and Tim _____ read many books.
5 Karen _____ walk to school, she goes by bicycle.
6 You _____ tidy your room very often.

4 (＊＊) John is a student at a summer school. Read his email to his friend Simon and correct the sentences.

> **To:**   simon@12gemail.com
> **From:**   john12@tmail.co.uk
> **Subject:** Summer school
>
> Hi Simon,
>
> Summer school is fantastic!! We get up at 9.00 a.m. every day, then we have lessons at 10.00 a.m. They're really easy! In the evening, we watch TV or play computer games – we don't have homework! We go to bed at about 11.00 p.m. The food here is great – tonight is hamburgers and chips. ☺
>
> Talk to you soon,
> John

1 John gets up at 7.00 a.m.
   He doesn't get up at 7.00 a.m.,
   he gets up at 9.00 a.m.
2 Lessons start at 8.00 a.m.
   _____
   _____
3 In the evenings, John does homework.
   _____
   _____
4 John goes to bed at 10.00 p.m.
   _____
   _____
5 John doesn't like the food at summer school.
   _____
   _____

5 (✱✱) **Put the words in the correct order to make sentences.**

1 alone/Emma/live/doesn't

Emma doesn't live alone.

2 chocolate/eat/don't/I

_____ .

3 long/read/don't/they/books

_____ .

4 hair/my/like/doesn't/brother/his

_____ .

5 wear/don't/parents/glasses/my

_____ .

6 doesn't/Mike/in/watch/bed/TV

_____ .

7 doesn't/to/school/cycle/Sam

_____ .

8 work/my/parents/don't/the weekends/at

_____ .

Object pronouns

6 (✱) **Underline the correct objects pronouns.**

1 I don't watch TV. I don't like _it/us/them_ very much.

2 She's mad about football. She always watches _them/it/him_ on TV.

3 Your parents aren't at home. Send _it/them/her_ a text message.

4 This homework is very difficult. Please help _us/them/our_!

5 I haven't got my keys. Have you got _them/us/it_?

6 She never helps her brother. She doesn't like _him/her/it_ very much.

7 (✱✱) **Complete the sentences with the correct object pronouns.**

1 Is this your new MP3 player? I really like _it_ .

2 James isn't friendly. I don't like ___ .

3 Have you got your photos? I want to see ___ .

4 She always drinks cola. She loves ___ .

5 My computer is broken. Please send ___ a text message.

6 Miss Robson is my Science teacher. I really like ___ .

Grammar reference

Present simple negative

Form

| – | I/You/We/They **do not (don't) live**
He/She/It **does not (doesn't) live** | in France. |

I **don't walk** to school.
We **don't like** Maths.
He **doesn't play** computer games.

Subject and object pronouns

Subject pronouns	Object pronouns
I	me
you	you
he	him
she	her
it	it
we	us
you	you
they	them

We use object pronouns when we don't want to name the object.

I don't like **Tom**.
I don't like **him**. (him = Tom)

I often go to the cinema with **Ann**.
I often go to the cinema with **her**. (her = Ann)

I wear **school uniform** every day.
I wear **it** every day. (it = school uniform)

Take **these books** to the library.
Take **them** to the library. (them = these books)

Vocabulary
Free time

1 Match the words in column A with a word or phrase in column B.

A		B	
1	listen	a	sport
2	read	b	to the cinema
3	hang out	c	at home
4	go	d	to music
5	help	e	books
6	do	f	with friends

2 Complete the sentences with the correct words.

1 I usually l _i_ _s_ _t_ _e_ _n_ to music on my MP3 player.

2 We often h _ _ p our parents at the weekend.

3 Helena often _ _ _ ds books in the evening.

4 All students at our school _ _ sport in the afternoon.

5 We usually _ _ s _ t relatives on Sundays.

6 I sometimes go s _ o _ _ _ ng on Saturdays.

3 Complete the sentences about Sandra's weekend with the words below.

> hang out   lunch   piano   listen to ✓
> the cinema   visit

Teen World

| Home | Advice | Blogs | Quizzes | Games | Entertainment |

Sandra's Blog – July 24

My weekend

I'm always busy at the weekend. On Saturday morning I have a dancing lesson. In the afternoon, I ¹ _listen to_ music or ² _____ with my friends – we often go to ³ _____ .

On Sundays, I go with my family to ⁴ _____ relatives – we usually have ⁵ _____ together. Then in the afternoon I have a ⁶ _____ lesson. My uncle is a great music teacher.

Sandra

Grammar
Present simple questions

4 (✱) Complete the conversation between Dan and Ana. Use *do* or *does*.

Dan: ¹ _Do_ you see your boyfriend every day?

Ana: No, I don't but I phone him every day.

Dan: ² ___ he go to school with you?

Ana: Yes, he ³ ___ but we're in different classes.

Dan: Where ⁴ ___ you and your boyfriend go out? Do you often go to the cinema?

Ana: Yes, we ⁵ ___ . We love films!

Dan: ⁶ ___ your boyfriend play football?

Ana: Yes, he ⁷ ___ . He plays every Saturday!

Dan: Do you watch football?

Ana: No, I ⁸ ___ . I hate football!

5 (✱✱) Put the words in the correct order to make questions. Then write short answers.

1 like/coffee/you/do/? (✗)

   Do you like coffee?
   No, I don't.

2 Peter/football/does/play/? (✓)

   _____

   _____

3 Madrid/does/in/Leona/live/? (✗)

   _____

   _____

4 your/do/parents/tennis/play/? (✓)

   _____

   _____

5 Frank/by bus/does/go/to school/? (✗)

   _____

   _____

6 you/study/Chinese/do/? (✓)

   _____

   _____

6 (✱) **Match questions 1–6 with answers a–f.**

1 How old is Peter?   a At 7.15.
2 What time does Nico get up?   b By bus.
3 Where is the cinema?   c Every day.
4 How often does Tim phone you?   d He's fifteen.
5 Are you a student?   e It's in the city centre.
6 How do you go to school?   f Yes, I am.

7 (✱✱) **Complete the questions with the correct question word:** *Where, How, What time, When* **or** *How often.*

1 *Where* do you live?
I live in Manchester.
2 _____ is Manchester?
It's in England.
3 _____ do you have PE lessons?
Every day.
4 _____ do you wake up in the morning?
At seven o'clock.
5 _____ do you go to school?
By bike – and sometimes I walk.
6 _____ do you do your homework?
In the evening after school.

8 (✱✱) **Read the dialogue. Put the words in the correct order to make questions.**

Marco: Hi! I'm Marco!
Pete: Hi, Marco! I'm Pete. I'm from the UK ¹you/are/Where/from?
Marco: *Where are you from?*
Pete: I'm from Italy. ²music/do you/What/like?
Marco: _____
Pete: I like rock and heavy metal.
Marco: I like rock, too. ³you/do/at the weekend/What/do?
_____
Pete: I hang out with friends – we often go shopping or to the cinema. ⁴football/like/you/Do? _____
Marco: Yes! I love football! Especially AC Milan. ⁵football/play/you/Do?
_____
Pete: Yes, I play football at weekends and I watch it on TV.
⁶do/you/How often/visit this chat site? _____
_____
Marco: Every day! Speak to you soon!

Grammar reference

Present simple questions

Form

?	Do I/you/we/they **like** Does he/she/it **like**	music?

Short answers	Yes, I/you/we/they **do**. No, I/you/we/they **don't**. Yes, he/she/it **does**. No, he/she/it **doesn't**.

Wh- questions

To form *wh-* questions we add a question word (*where, what, what time, when, how, why, how often*) at the beginning of a question.

Where *do you study?*
At university.

What *do they have for lunch?*
Soup or pasta.

What time *does she go to bed?*
At 11 p.m.

When *do your lessons start?*
At 8 a.m.

How *does he get to school?*
By bus.

Why *do you go to the library every day?*
Because I like reading.

How often *does Ann have lunch at school?*
Once a week.

self-assessment test 1

Vocabulary & Grammar

1 Write the words with the opposite meaning.

1 girlfriend   _boyfriend_
2 grandmother   _____
3 men   _____
4 tall   _____
5 dark hair   _____

/4

2 Complete the sentences with one word in each gap.

1 Mr Smith has got two children: his son is twelve and his d _a_ _u_ _g_ _h_ _t_ _e_ _r_ is fifteen.
2 I've got a p _ _ _ _ _ of tissues in my bag.
3 My Maths teacher has got a moustache but he hasn't got a b _ _ _ _ .
4 I haven't got my ID c _ _ _ with me.
5 Robert has got £5 in his w _ _ _ _ _ .

/4

3 Underline the word that you cannot use with the words in bold.

1 **start** lessons/the classroom/school
2 **go** to the library/for a walk/to music
3 **do** uniform/homework/sport
4 **get** dressed/school/up
5 **study** school/science/languages
6 **go** by bus/home/lunch

/5

4 Complete the sentences with the correct form of the verbs in brackets.

1 I _don't like_ (not like) chewing gum.
2 Nick often _____ (watch) TV after school.
3 I _____ (not have got) a pet.
4 Bethany and Matthew _____ (wake up) late on Saturdays.
5 My dad _____ (not help) me with my homework.
6 We _____ (not cycle) to school every day.
7 My best friend _____ (have got) two mobile phones.

/6

5 Choose the correct option a, b or c, to complete the sentences.

1 Where is ___ hairbrush?
   a me   b my ✓   c mine
2 What's your ___ name?
   a cousin   b cousin's   c cousins'
3 ___ a packet of tissues in your bag?
   a Is there   b There is   c There isn't
4 This is ___ house.
   a us   b ours   c our
5 ___ three pens on her desk.
   a There is   b Are   c There are
6 The TV is in my ___ room. They watch it every day.
   a parents   b parents'   c parent's
7 I never eat bananas. I don't like ___ .
   a them   b they   c their

/6

6 Complete the questions with the verbs below in the correct form. Then match the questions with the answers.

read   play   have   visit   finish ✓
hang out

1 ☐ What time _do you finish_ (you) school?
2 ☐ How often _____ (she) with friends?
3 ☐ What _____ (they) for breakfast?
4 ☐ When _____ (Robert) relatives?
5 ☐ Where _____ (your friends) football?
6 ☐ What books _____ (you) in your free time?

a I like Lord of the Rings books.
b Once a week.
c In the park near our school.
d At 3.30 pm. ✓
e Orange juice and toast.
f At the weekend.

/5

20

Reading

7 Read the website for teenagers who want to make new friends. Then complete the sentences with the correct names.

teen bloggers

My name is Hannah but my friends call me Shorty because I'm very short. I'm fifteen years old and live with my parents, my sister Ella and our cat Flossy. After school I usually hang out with friends and go shopping! And I often buy small things: a new hairbrush, lip salve or chewing gum.

Hi! I'm Tim and I'm fourteen. I often read books and go to the cinema with Fiona, my sister. I sometimes watch films on TV and play computer games. I've got a lot of books, computer games and magazines in my room. It's a complete mess! I like school. I love History and Geography but PE is not my thing at all!.

I'm sixteen and my name is Alice. I'm football mad. Sometimes I go to bed and watch football matches in my room at night. And the next day I start school at 8 a.m.! I always walk or cycle so I'm often late! School is OK and I like my teachers, too. They are really nice.

Hello everybody! It's Nick here. I'm good-looking and fun! :-) I live in Bournemouth with my parents and my little brother Tom. I think Bournemouth is a fantastic town. My grandparents and my cousins live here too and I go to their house by bus three times a week. They love animals and they've got a dog called Bobby. At weekends I play the guitar and the piano and listen to my MP3 player.

1 _____ often visits her/his relatives.
2 _____ has got TV in her/his room.
3 _____ never goes to school by bus.
4 _____'s things are not tidy.
5 _____ has got a nickname.
6 _____ likes music.
7 _____ doesn't like sport.
8 _____ has got a pet.

/8

Listening

8 (2) Listen to the conversation between Jane and her aunt Beth. Tick (✓) true or cross (✗) false.

1 ☐ Jane doesn't like her new History teacher.
2 ☐ There are thirteen boys in Jane's class.
3 ☐ Matthew has got one brother.
4 ☐ Matthew's aunt is an Art teacher at Jane and Matthew's school.
5 ☐ Jane and Matthew have Art three times a week.
6 ☐ Matthew doesn't like Art.
7 ☐ Matthew is good at French.

/7

Communication

9 Complete the sentences with one word in each gap. Then match the sentences with suitable answers.

1 [e] Have you got _brothers_ or sisters?
2 ☐ _____ is my boyfriend, Ian.
3 ☐ How _____ is your sister?
4 ☐ Is this your first _____ in the UK?
5 ☐ _____ are you from?
6 ☐ What's your _____ football team?

a I'm from Prague.
b She's eighteen.
c It's Chelsea.
d Pleased to meet you.
e I've got two sisters. ✓
f No, it isn't. But it's my first time in London.

/5

Marks

Vocabulary & Grammar	/30 marks
Reading	/8 marks
Listening	/7 marks
Communication	/5 marks
Total:	/50 marks

Vocabulary

Shopping

1 Match the objects 1–8 with the shops a–h.

1 magazine
2 jeans
3 make-up
4 paper
5 CD
6 banana
7 bread
8 trainers

a clothes shop
b newsagent's
c baker's
d stationer's
e shoe shop
f greengrocer's
g pharmacy
h music shop

2 Complete the crossword.

Across

5 You eat food in a _____ .

7 You buy fruit and vegetables at a _____ .

Down

1 I go to the _____ to get medicine.

2 You buy pens, pencils, paper, cards and diaries at a _____ shop.

3 My sister buys her magazines at the _____ .

4 A _____ makes bread.

6 I often buy CDs at the _____ shop.

Grammar

Countable and uncountable nouns

3 (*) Put the words in the correct column.

> rain ✓   key   diary   banana   perfume
> music   bread   pen   make-up   mirror

countable	uncountable
	rain

4 (*) Complete the sentences with *a* or *some*.

1 Ben is in the stationer's. He wants to buy
_a_ diary.

2 Rosa has got _____ new trainers.

3 There is _____ brown bread on the table.

4 I've got _____ great music on my MP3 player.

5 Is there _____ hairbrush in your bag?

6 It isn't cold today but there is _____ rain.

some/any

5 (**) Write sentences about Jay's bag of shopping. Use *a*, *some* or *any*.

1 *There is some bread.* _____ (bread)
2 *There aren't any magazines.* (magazines)
3 _____ (bottle of shampoo)
4 _____ (purse)
5 _____ (chocolate)
6 _____ (MP3 player)
7 _____ (book)
8 _____ (chewing gum)

6 (★★) **Write questions with *a* or *any*. Then write short answers.**

1 children/park (✗)

Are there any children in the park?
No, there aren't.

2 people/shopping mall (✓)

_____

_____

3 sugar/my coffee (✗)

_____

_____

4 Chinese restaurant/your town (✓)

_____

_____

5 bookshelf/classroom (✗)

_____

_____

6 traffic/town centre (✓)

_____

_____

7 (★) **Complete the phone conversation between Tom and Liz. Use *a*, *some*, or *any*.**

Tom: Hi Liz!

Liz: Hi Tom. Where are you?

Tom: I'm in the park. I'm with ¹_____ friends. There's ²_____ football game today. Where are you?

Liz: I'm in the town centre. There's ³_____ new shopping mall in the town centre. It's great!

Tom: A new shopping mall? Are there ⁴_____ good sports shops?

Liz: Yes, there's ⁵_____ good sports shop and ⁶_____ great clothes shops.

Tom: Are there ⁷_____ restaurants?

Liz: Yes, there's ⁸_____ French restaurant.

Grammar Plus: Plural spelling

8 (★) **Complete the sentences. Write the plural form of the words in brackets.**

1 I've got some good *friends* in the USA. (friend)

2 There are five _____ on the table. (glass)

3 Are there any _____ in the house? (woman)

4 There are ten _____ in the garden. (person)

5 Has Mia got any _____ in her bag? (tomato)

6 There are four _____ on the table. (box)

Grammar reference

Countable and uncountable nouns; *some/any*

Countable nouns

Countable nouns can be singular or plural (*a shop, shops; a book, books*).

We use plural countable nouns with *some* (in affirmative sentences) and *any* (in negative sentences and questions) to talk about quantity.

*There are **some** nice <u>cafés</u> in my town.*
*I've got **some** <u>CDs</u> in my bedroom.*
*We haven't got **any** <u>apples</u>.*
*Are there **any** good <u>cinemas</u> here?*

We don't use *some* or *any* with singular countable nouns; we use *a*.

*I've got **a** <u>cat</u>.*
*There isn't **a** <u>wardrobe</u> in our bedroom.*
*Have you got **a** <u>gift</u> for her?*

Spelling of plural nouns

• With most nouns, we add -*s*.

cat → cats, apple → apples

• With nouns ending in a consonant + *y*, change to -*ies*.

city → cities, lady → ladies

• With nouns ending in -*ch*, -*sh*, -*s*, -*x* and some ending in -*o*, add -*es*.

match → matches, dish → dishes, class → classes, fox → foxes, potato → potatoes

• With nouns ending in -*fe*, change to -*ves*.

wife → wives, knife → knives, life → lives

• Important irregular nouns are:

man → men, woman → women, child → children, person → people, foot → feet, tooth → teeth

Uncountable nouns

Uncountable nouns are always singular (*water, music, traffic*).

We can use them with *some* (in affirmative sentences) and *any* (in negative sentences and questions) to talk about quantity.

*There is **some** <u>milk</u> in the fridge.*
*I've got **some** <u>chocolate</u>.*
*There isn't **any** <u>traffic</u> today.*
*Have you got **any** <u>shampoo</u>?*

+	There's **some** water.
–	There isn't **any** water.
?	Is there **any** water?

Vocabulary

My home

1 Find the home words in the word square.
Look ➜ and ⬇ .

> cooker ✓   sink   wardrobe   chair
> bed   cupboard   bath

s	c	o	o	k	e	r	o	a
i	b	a	d	g	h	k	l	r
n	a	g	s	d	v	n	m	m
k	t	a	j	i	m	n	b	c
e	h	c	a	d	f	g	n	h
c	u	p	b	o	a	r	d	a
b	j	k	o	u	o	p	l	i
a	b	b	e	d	b	g	n	r
t	d	b	m	i	o	p	s	z
h	w	a	r	d	r	o	b	e

2 Complete the text about Jo's bedroom with the words below.

> flat ✓   bed   living room   bedroom
> bookcase   wardrobe

| People ▼ | Search |

Home   Browse   Find people   Forums   Music   More   **My homepage ▼**

My room

My family live in a small ¹ _flat_ . I've got
one brother, David. I haven't got any
sisters. David's ² _____ is always
messy! Mine is always tidy. I've got a
small ³ _____ – but it's really
comfortable to sleep in, a ⁴ _____
for my clothes and a big ⁵ _____
with lots of books because I love reading!
I haven't got a TV in my bedroom. The TV
is in the ⁶ _____ .

Grammar

much/many/a lot of

3 (✱) <u>Underline</u> the correct words to complete
the sentences.

1 Harry doesn't play football in the garden.
There isn't *many/<u>much</u>* space.

2 Melanie doesn't wear *many/much* make-up.

3 There aren't *many/much* restaurants in
my town.

4 Brad hasn't got *many/much* books. He
doesn't read very often.

5 Lily usually sits on the floor to watch TV.
There aren't *many/much* armchairs in the
living room.

6 My bedroom is very small. There isn't
many/much space for my things.

4 (✱) Complete the questions with *How much* or
How many. Then answer the questions.

1 _How many_ rooms are there in your house?

2 _____ books are there in your bedroom?

3 _____ money do you get from your
parents every month?

4 _____ people are there in your family?

5 _____ space is there in your house?

6 _____ subjects do you study?

5 (✱✱) Write questions with *How much* or
How many.

1 money/purse
How much money is there in your
purse?

2 students/your class
_____ ?

3 contacts/your mobile phone
_____ ?

4 space/your bedroom
_____ ?

5 rain/your country
_____ ?

6 shops/your town
_____ ?

6 (✱) **Look at the questions. Choose the correct short answers.**

1 Have you got a lot of rooms in your flat?
  a No, not many. ✓
  b No, not much.

2 Have you got much homework tonight?
  a No, not many.
  b No, not much.

3 Have you got a lot of clothes?
  a No, not very many.
  b No, not very much.

4 Is there a lot of rain in the summer?
  a No, there aren't very many.
  b No, there isn't very much.

7 (✱✱) **Look at the picture of Bill's room and write sentences with** *much/many/a lot of*. **Use the ideas below.**

> space   clothes ✓   posters   books   CDs   furniture
> shoes

There are a lot of clothes.
There aren't many ...

_____
_____
_____
_____
_____

Grammar reference

much/many/a lot of

We use *much, many* and *a lot of* to talk about quantity.

Much

We use *much* with uncountable nouns in negative sentences, questions and negative short answers.

*I haven't got **much** money.*
*How **much** sugar do you want?*
*Not **much**.*

Many

We use *many* with plural countable nouns in negative sentences, questions and negative short answers.

*She hasn't got **many** friends.*
*How **many** CDs have you got?*
*Not **many**.*

A lot of

We use *a lot of* with uncountable nouns and plural countable nouns in affirmative and negative sentences.

*There's **a lot of** traffic here.*
*We've got **a lot of** sweets.*
*There isn't **a lot of** homework for tomorrow.*
*We haven't got **a lot of** eggs in the fridge.*

> **Notice!**
> I read ***a lot of** books*.
> I read ***a lot***.

Vocabulary

In town

1 Match the activities with the places in town.

1	leave your car	a	stadium
2	read a book	b	restaurant
3	surf	c	post office
4	see a film	d	beach
5	see famous paintings	e	cinema
6	buy stamps or postcards	f	library
7	eat dinner	g	art gallery
8	watch a football match	h	car park

2 Complete the text with the words below.

> sports centre   polluted   beautiful ✓
> markets   fantastic   terrible   university

COOL CITIES
Home

Edinburgh

I'm from Edinburgh in Scotland. It's a ¹ _beautiful_ old city. I love Edinburgh because there are lots of things to do. The weather is sometimes ² _____ – cold and wet, but you can visit museums or go to the ³ _____ shops and department stores when the weather is bad!

There is a very good ⁴ _____ in the city. Lots of students love to come to Edinburgh to study. The students like the great restaurants and cafés – they are not expensive! Edinburgh has some interesting ⁵ _____ – they sell lots of different things – clothes, books, jewellery …

There is a great ⁶ _____ in the city. It has a big swimming pool and lots of people do sport there. I go swimming once a week. Edinburgh is not ⁷ _____ – it is near beautiful countryside with mountains and lakes.

Mohammed

Reading

3 Look at the photos in the leaflet about summer school cities. Do you know any of these places?

SUMMER SCHOOL CITIES

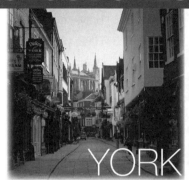

York is a beautiful city in the north of England. There are some beautiful old buildings in York and lots of interesting art galleries and cafés. The weather is often bad, it can be cold and rainy but it isn't an expensive city.

YORK

BRIGHTON

Brighton is a young and exciting place. The music scene is brilliant in Brighton and in the evening you can go to some great clubs. Brighton has got a fantastic beach and the weather is often good.

London is a very large, multicultural city. There is a lot to do in London. There are brilliant theatres and cinemas. It has also got fantastic shops and restaurants and you can eat food from all over the world. It is an expensive city and the traffic is terrible. The weather is good but there is a lot of pollution.

LONDON

CAMBRIDGE

This is a famous and beautiful city. It is very popular with tourists. It has got a very famous university and there are lots of students. There are lots of interesting bookshops and cafés. There are about eighty parks in Cambridge and traffic isn't a problem in the city centre – cars do not go in the city centre but cyclists can! The weather is usually good, it's often sunny.

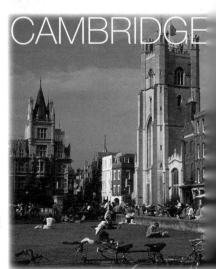

4 Read the leaflet. Tick (✓) true or cross (✗) false.

1 ☐ The weather in York is good.
2 ☐ York is an expensive city.
3 ☐ There is a beach in Brighton.
4 ☐ There is not a lot to do in the evening in Brighton.
5 ☐ You can eat food from lots of different countries in London.
6 ☐ The weather is bad in London.
7 ☐ There are a lot of tourists in Cambridge.
8 ☐ The weather is often bad in Cambridge.

5 Read the sentences and write where the speakers are: York (Y), Brighton (B), London (L) or Cambridge (C).

1 ☐ It is great for cycling and clean air!
2 ☐ I'm glad I've got my umbrella with me!
3 ☐ You can have Chinese food, Thai, Greek, Turkish – there is so much choice.
4 ☐ I can sit on the beach and read all day, it's brilliant.
5 ☐ Everything is very cheap here, I love it.
6 ☐ In the park there are hundreds of students studying in the sunshine.
7 ☐ I dance every night, so I'm tired every day!

6 Read what these students say. Write the best city for Lucy, Fred, Jane and Jonathon.

1 Lucy: _____

> *I want to be in the countryside. I don't like big cities or traffic.*

2 Luca: _____

> *I haven't got much money so I don't want to go to an expensive city. I study History and Art in my free time.*

3 Jane: _____

> *I spend a lot of time in shops. I go out a lot in the evenings and I often eat in restaurants. I like big cities.*

4 Joshua: _____

> *I listen to music a lot and dance in clubs. I like exciting cities. I don't like bad weather.*

Listening

7 Look at the photograph. Where is Lucy's summer school?

8 ⟨3⟩ Listen to the conversation between Lucy and her friend, Jill. Match the words in the box to the adjectives.

> college ✓   buildings   city   bedrooms
> people   restaurants

a beautiful   *college*
b small   _____
c famous   _____
d interesting   _____
e not exciting   _____
f fantastic   _____

9 ⟨3⟩ Listen again and choose the correct answer.

1 Lucy describes her summer school as
   a brilliant.   b not brilliant.   c terrible.
2 In Cambridge there is
   a a lot of traffic and pollution.
   b no traffic only bikes.
   c not a lot of traffic.
3 Lucy says there are
   a lots of famous buildings but no parks.
   b lots of parks and famous buildings.
   c lots of parks and lots of bikes.
4 Lucy goes to the bookshops and cafés and
   a buys books.   b drinks tea.
   c buys books and has coffee.
5 In the evenings Lucy
   a goes to bookshops and cafés.
   b eats in restaurants.
   c meets other students and studies English.
6 Why doesn't Lucy go to restaurants?
   a She hasn't got much money.
   b There aren't any.   c She has to study.

Writing

A note to a friend

1 Write the name of the person you are writing to: *Anna, Hi John,*

2 Make a suggestion: *Let's go to the cinema, Come to the park, Can you meet me?*

> Janet,
>
> Let's go shopping on Saturday. There's a new shopping mall near the market.
>
> See you at the bus stop at 10.00 a.m.
>
> Can you come? Give me a call or send me a text.
>
> Rachel

3 Arrange a place and a time to meet: *See you at the cinema at 6.00 p.m, The address is … , Let's meet at 2.00 p.m.*

4 Ask for confirmation: *Can you come? Send me a text.*

5 Sign your name: *Liz, Neil, Rachel*

---

1 Read the note and answer the questions.

1 Where does Rachel want to go?

_____

2 When does she want to go?

_____

3 What time does she want to meet?

_____

4 Where does she want to meet?

_____

2 Read the note and replace the <u>underlined</u> phrases with a phrase below.

[Call me.   The address is   Let's go ✓
See you]

○ Julian
○
○ ¹ <u>Come</u> / <u>Let's go</u> to the new club
○ on Saturday.
○
○ There's a new band. ² <u>The club is at</u> /
○   _____ 50 Wellington Street.
○
○ ³ <u>Let's meet</u> / _____ at my house
○ at 4.00 p.m.
○
○ Can you come? ⁴ <u>Send me a text.</u> /
○   _____
○
○ John

3 Sentences 1–6 are very long. Match them with the short phrases a–f.

1 I have a new mobile phone and you can text me on that. The number is 788 6536479.

2 Dear Sarah,

3 The film starts at 7.30 p.m. so my idea is to meet at 7.15. We can meet outside the cinema.

4 Do you want to come to the cinema with me?

5 Do you know where the cinema is? Let me tell you. It is in town and the address is 15 Galway Road.

6 You know I love horror films and I think that there is a good film on tonight.

a The address is 15 Galway Road.

b There's a good horror film on tonight.

c My number is 788 6536479, send me a text.

d Sarah,

e Let's go to the cinema.

f See you at 7.15 outside the cinema.

4 **a** <u>Underline</u> the important information in Peter's note.

> Dear Andy,
>
> How are you? I'm fine. <u>I want to go to the new youth club on Sunday, do you want to come?</u> There is a new music band and I like to see new bands. Do you know where the new club is? Here is the address – 60 High Farm Road. I live near there so we can meet at my house. I think 6.00 is a good time. Do you think you can come? Maybe you can call me?
>
> That's all for now
>
> Peter.

b Rewrite Peter's note using just the underlined important information. Use the short phrases from exercise 3 to help you.

Let's go to the new youth club on Sunday.

_____
_____
_____
_____
_____

5 Put the phrases below into the correct category.

> Let's meet at 7.00.   See you at the bus stop.
> Come to the concert with me. ✓
> See you at 10.00.   Let's go to the cinema.
> The address is 4 Old Road.

Suggestions

1 *Come to the concert with me.*
2 _____

Where to meet

3 _____
4 _____

Time to meet

5 _____
6 _____

6 Complete the strategies box with the phrases below.

> at the park   Send me a text!
> Can you come? ✓   the cinema at 8 p.m.

Writing a note

- Make a suggestion: *Let's go to …* ,
  1 *Can you come?*
- Arrange when and where to meet: *Let's meet*
  2 _____ .
- Remember to include a time: *See you outside*
  3 _____
- Ask for confirmation: 4 _____
- Remember to sign your name.

7 Read the task and then write your note. Use the strategies in exercise 6 to help you.

> You want to go to a music concert on Friday. Write a note to your partner.
> - Make the suggestion.
> - Say a time and place to meet.
> - Ask for confirmation.

Speaking

Asking for directions

8 Use the diagrams to complete the dialogue.

1 A: Excuse me. How do I get to the Post Office?

B: Let me see. 1 *turn right* into Elm Street. Then 2 _____ . Then take the 3 _____ into Baker Street. You can't miss it.

A: Thank you very much.

2 A: Excuse me. How do I get to the art gallery?

B: 4 _____ King Street. Then take the 5 _____ , that's Ash Road. Take the 6 _____ and the gallery is there.

9 Complete the dialogues with the phrases below.

> turn   Can   miss   excuse me ✓
> straight   get   take   here

1 A: 1 *Excuse me* . How do I 2 _____ to the train station?

B: You 3 _____ left into Drum Street. Then you 4 _____ the second right into Harly Road.

A: 5 _____ you say that again?

B: Yes, Harly Road.

A: OK, right into Harly Road.

B: Yes, and then go 6 _____ on, and it is on the right. You can't 7 _____ it.

A: Is it near 8 _____ ?

B: Oh yes, it is a short walk.

A: Thank you very much.

> near ✓   can't   down   Thank you
> first   turn left

2 A: Excuse me. Is the History Museum 1 *near* here?

B: Yes it is. Take the 2 _____ right into King Street. Then 3 _____ at the Post Office.

A: Go 4 _____ St John's Street and the History Museum is in front of you.

B: Is it a big museum?

A: Yes, it's a big glass square, you 5 _____ miss it.

B: 6 _____ very much.

urban life

29

* easy to do
** a bit harder

Vocabulary

Sport

1 Label the sports.

karate   gymnastics ✓   baseball   rugby
badminton   rowing   judo   basketball

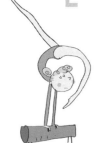  

1 _gymnastics_   2 _____   3 _____

4 _____   5 _____   6 _____

7 _____   8 _____

2 Complete the sentences with *go*, *do* or *play*.

1 John doesn't _do_ gymnastics very often.
2 Do you _____ skiing in the winter?
3 Jack is very tall but he can't _____
   basketball very well.
4 How often do you _____ swimming?
5 Martin and Martha _____ running every
   morning.
6 Sylvie and Kate _____ badminton at the
   sports centre.
7 Tom and Alex often _____ judo in the
   afternoon.

Grammar

can

3 (*) Look at the table. Complete the sentences with *can* and *can't*.

	Leo	John	Ann
play the piano	✓	✗	✗
speak French	✓	✗	✓
do karate	✗	✗	✓
swim	✓	✓	✓
cook well	✗	✗	✗
ski	✓	✓	✗

1 Leo _can_ play the piano.
2 Ann and Leo _____ speak French.
3 John and Leo _____ do karate.
4 Ann _____ swim.
5 John and Ann _____ play the piano.
6 Ann _____ do karate.
7 Leo, John and Ann _____ swim.

4 (**) Write questions. Use the information in exercise 3 to answer the questions. Then write short answers.

1 Ann/swim?
   Can Ann swim?
   Yes, she can.
2 Ann and Leo/speak French?
   _____
   _____
3 Leo/play piano?
   _____
   _____
4 John and Leo/do karate?
   _____
   _____
5 John/cook well?
   _____
   _____
6 Leo and John/ski?
   _____
   _____

5 (✱✱) Put the words in the correct order to make sentences.

1 Spanish/can/I/speak

I can speak Spanish.

2 grandfather/play/tennis/can/my

_____ .

3 Sam/the/can/play/piano

_____ .

4 Japanese/speak/can/teacher/my

_____ .

5 Natasha/run/can/five/kilometres

_____ .

6 my friends/the/can/dance/tango

_____ .

7 Emma/speak/can/French

_____ .

8 can/do/I/gymnastics

_____ .

6 (✱✱) Rewrite the sentences. Put the words in brackets in the correct place.

1 I play the piano very well. (can't)

I can't play the piano very well.

2 My sister can swim. (quite well)

_____

3 Can you play rugby? (well)

_____

4 My grandmother walk very well. (can't)

_____

5 Can your sister sing? (well)

_____

6 Dan and Kim dance quite well. (can)

_____

7 My brother plays tennis very well. (can't)

_____

8 I can ski. (quite well)

_____

7 (✱✱) How well can you do these things? Write sentences using *can/can't* with *very/quite well*.

> speak English   dance   play tennis   ski   cook
> sing   swim   play the piano

1 _____
2 _____
3 _____
4 _____
5 _____
6 _____
7 _____
8 _____

Grammar reference

can – ability

Form

+	I/You/He/She/It/We/They **can**	play
–	I/You/He/She/It/We/They **can't**	tennis.
?	**Can** I/you/he/she/it/we/they	play tennis?

Short answers	Yes, I/you/he/she/it/we/they **can**. No, I/you/he/she/it/we/they **can't**.

Wh- questions	Answers
What can you do?	I can play tennis.

Use

We use *can* to talk about ability.

*I **can** swim.*
*My sister **can't** dance.*
***Can** you run fast?*

We use *very well, well, quite well* with *can* to say *how* well we can do something.

*Our teacher **can** speak English **very well**.*
*Robert **can** play tennis **well**.*
*I **can** ride a motorbike **quite well**.*

We use *well* and *very well* with *can't*.

*We **can't** sing (**very**) well.*
*I **can't** drive a car (**very**) well.*

> **Notice!**
>
> We do not use *quite well* in negative sentences.

Vocabulary

Health

1 Label the parts of the body.

> head   toe   foot   shoulder   hand ✓
> arm   knee   ankle   stomach   leg
> elbow   finger   neck

2 _____

1 _hand_

3 _____

4 _____

5 _____

6 _____

13 _____

7 _____

10 _____   9 _____

8 _____

11 _____

12 _____

2 <u>Underline</u> the correct words to complete the sentences.

1 I've got *a sore leg/<u>stomachache</u>* and I don't want to eat.

2 She can't play the piano very well because she's got *a sore throat/a pain* in her hand.

3 John's got *a toothache/backache*. He doesn't want any ice-cream.

4 I'm sorry, I can't sing very well. I've got *a sore throat/a pain in my arm*.

5 Brenda can't run very fast because she's got *an earache/a pain in her knee*.

6 I've got a stomachache and I can't eat. I *feel sick/have got a cough*.

Grammar

Adverbs of manner

3 (✱✱) Make adverbs from the adjectives below and complete the sentences.

> loud   hard   slow ✓   careful   quick
> clear

1 I've got a sore foot so I walk _slowly_ .

2 Ali can't sing _____ . He's got a sore throat.

3 Jessica's got a pain in her leg. She can't walk _____ .

4 Miss Lane is a good teacher. She explains things _____ .

5 Elena is a good student. She always works _____ .

6 My mum is a good driver. She always drives _____ .

4 (✱) Complete the text with the correct form of the words in brackets.

| People ▼ | Search |

Home   Browse   Find people   Forums   Music   More   My homepage ▼

<u>My brother</u>

My brother Thomas is disabled. He uses an electric wheelchair because he can't walk. He can move very [1] _____ (fast) in his wheelchair. He plays wheelchair basketball with his friends. He can play very [2] _____ (good). Thomas writes for a sports magazine. He works very [3] _____ (hard) on his computer at home. He types very [4] _____ (quick). He works in the living room at home. He always plays music [5] _____ (loud). Thomas has got a special car. He is a good driver and he drives very [6] _____ (careful).

Grammar Plus: Position of adverbs

5 (**) Put the words in the correct order to make sentences.

1 very fast/runs/she

She runs very fast.

2 can/play/the piano/very well/I

_____ .

3 he/makes friends/easily/very

_____ .

4 swim/can/well/I

_____ .

5 baby/gently/hold/the

_____ .

6 carefully/to/listen/the teacher

_____ .

Imperatives

6 (*) Match the problems 1–6 with the advice a–f.

Problems

1 I always feel tired.
2 I can't see very well.
3 I've got a headache.
4 I haven't got any money.
5 I can't do my homework.
6 I've got a pain in my knee and my back.

Advice

a Drink lots of water and take some medicine.
b Do some exercise every day and go to bed early.
c Phone your friends and ask for help.
d Don't do any exercise today and go to see the doctor.
e Get some glasses.
f Try to find a job and earn some money.

7 (*) Complete the advice with *don't* or – .

How to do an English speaking test: TIPS

1 _Don't_ go to bed late.
2 _____ be nervous.
3 _____ listen to your teacher carefully.
4 _____ speak clearly.
5 _____ speak quickly.
6 _____ speak sadly, speak happily.

Grammar reference

Adverbs of manner

Form

Adjective	Adverb
slow	slowly
loud	loudly
clear	clearly
bad	badly

- With adjectives ending in *-y*, *-y* becomes *-ily*:

easy → easily, happy → happily

- Some adverbs are the same as adjectives:

hard → hard, fast → fast, late → late

- Other irregular adverbs:

good → well

Use

We use adverbs of manner with verbs to talk about <u>how</u> we do something.

*My grandmother walks **very slowly**.*
(*walks → how? → very slowly*)

*They run **quickly**.* (*run → how? → quickly*)

*She speaks English **well**.* (*speaks English → how? → well*)

*You swim **fast**.* (*swim → how? → fast*)

Position of adverbs

We usually put adverbs <u>after</u> the verb or verb + object.

*She <u>sings</u> **beautifully**.*
*I <u>ride a horse</u> **very well**.*

Imperatives

Form

Affirmative	Negative
Drink it.	*Don't drink it.*
Sing a song.	*Don't sing a song.*
Go to school.	*Don't go to school.*

Use

We use imperatives to give advice or instructions.

***Talk** to your mother about it.* (advice)
***Go** to bed and rest.* (advice)
***Do** your homework now.* (instructions)
***Don't touch** it.* (instructions)

Vocabulary

Extreme sports

1 Complete the crossword.

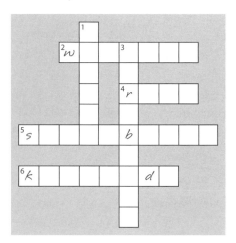

Across

2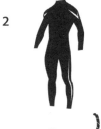

4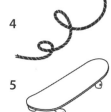

5

6

Down

1

3

2 Which equipment from exercise 1 do you use for these sports?

1 Cycling: *helmet*

2 Climbing: _____

3 Skating: _____

4 Surfing: _____

5 Diving: _____

6 Skateboarding: _____

Reading

Try a new sport!

What's on in your area
Meet the teachers and try something new

My name's David and I'm a surfing instructor. There are surfing lessons every weekday. We go to the beach in the morning with students before school. All the students wear wetsuits to surf because the water is usually cold. You need to bring your own surfboard. You can buy one at a good sports shop. A lot of my students can swim really well, but surfing is a difficult sport so my advice to new surfers is learn this sport slowly!

Surfing lessons Monday – Friday 7.00 a.m. – 8.00 a.m., West Point Beach

I'm Cheryl and I teach rock climbing. There are climbing classes for students on Saturday. It's great fun and you can make a lot of new friends. You don't need much equipment for climbing – just rope and we have some here at the centre, if you need some. You need to wear a helmet to protect your head but we have some here at the school and students can use them. Students always want to climb very fast but you need to practise a lot first. My advice to new climbers is warm up before you start and don't start climbing too fast. Climbing is hard work!

Climbing lessons Saturday – 3.30 p.m., Climbing Wall, East Road Sport Centre.

Hi! I'm Ryan. I'm a skateboarding instructor. I love my job because I love skateboarding! There are lessons here at the skate park every day after school and on Sundays. Skateboarding is very popular. All my students bring their own skateboards and many students also wear knee pads because you can hurt your knees easily. My advice to new skateboarders is: always wear a helmet. Skateboarding is a lot of fun but it is sometimes dangerous.

Skateboarding lessons
Sunday – Friday 4.30 p.m. – 6.30 p.m., Shaw Lane Skate Park.

3 Read the text and match each sentence with the correct sport: surfing, climbing or skateboarding.

1 There are lessons on Saturday. _____

2 There are no lessons at the weekend. _____

3 It's a good way to meet new people. _____

4 It's good to learn this sport slowly. _____

5 The centre has equipment if you need it. _____

6 You can hurt your knees. _____

7 It is sometimes dangerous. _____

8 Lessons are before school. _____

4 Read the text again and choose the correct answer.

1 There are surfing lessons
  a every day.
  b every weekday.
  c every weekend.

2 It's good to wear a wetsuit because the _____ is cold.
  a weather
  b water
  c beach

3 A lot of David's students
  a can swim really well.
  b can surf really well.
  c can swim really fast

4 The climbing centre has _____ for you to use.
  a equipment
  b special shoes
  c knee pads

5 Cheryl says climbing is
  a dangerous.
  b hard work.
  c slow.

6 All Ryan's students bring their own
  a helmets.
  b skateboards.
  c knee pads.

7 Ryan think skateboarding is
  a not difficult.
  b good fun.
  c very difficult.

8 When can you go to skateboarding lessons?
  a Saturday morning.
  b Monday morning.
  c Monday afternoon.

Listening

5 Look at the leaflet. What types of races are in the sports day?

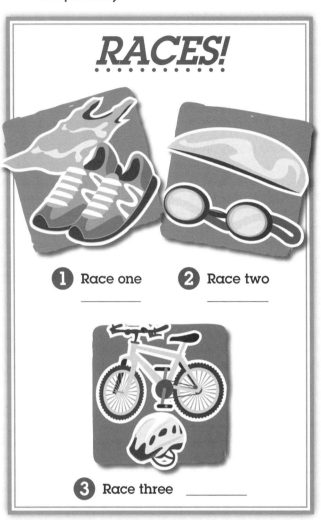

RACES!

1 Race one _____   **2** Race two _____

3 Race three _____

6 (4) Listen and tick (✓) true or cross (✗) false.

1 ☐ Race one is for boys and girls.

2 ☐ Only students age eighteen can run in race one.

3 ☐ Race two starts at 10.00 a.m.

4 ☐ Race two is 100 metres.

5 ☐ Race three starts at 3.00 p.m. today.

6 ☐ There are helmets for the cycling race in the blue tent.

7 (4) Listen again and match the statements to the correct race 1–3.

1 ☐ The race is 400 metres.

2 ☐ The race is tomorrow morning.

3 ☐ Only students from the school club can race.

4 ☐ You need to collect your number from the yellow tent.

5 ☐ You need to go to the sports centre at 9.45 a.m. tomorrow.

6 ☐ You need to wear protective equipment.

Reading

True/False

1 Read texts A, B and C. Tick (✓) true or cross (✗) false for sentences 1–6. In the false sentence, <u>underline</u> the wrong information.

A

> I like my town because there is a lot to do there. There are many restaurants and cafés, an interesting old museum and a great new sports centre.

1 ☐ The writer's town has got a lot of restaurants, a new museum and a sports centre.

2 ☐ The writer likes his town because you can go to cafes, visit a museum and do sports.

B

> I've got a brother and a sister. We like sports. We play badminton and tennis together every Saturday morning.

3 ☐ The writer often plays badminton with her sister and brother.

4 ☐ The writer plays badminton and tennis every morning.

C

> I live near to my school. I usually cycle to school but on Thursdays I walk with my friend, Amy.

5 ☐ The writer always cycles to school.

6 ☐ The writer doesn't cycle to school on Thursdays.

2 Read the text about Richard's life at Cambridge University. Tick (✓) true or cross (✗) false.

> I study Maths at Cambridge University. Life in Cambridge is a lot of fun. The town is beautiful. There are lots of old university buildings, great parks and more than twenty bridges over the River Cam. Lots of people go to work or university on their bikes.
>
> I live in my college with other students but I've got my own room with a bathroom. In the morning I go to lectures or study in the library. In the afternoon there are a lot of things to do. People say there is a club for everything at Cambridge University – and if there isn't, you can easily start one! I play in an orchestra and I'm also part of my college's rowing team. But some afternoons I just hang out at the pub with my friends or sit in a park … if the weather is good.

1 ☐ There are many beautiful new buildings in Cambridge.

2 ☐ Richard doesn't live in a room with other students.

3 ☐ There are a lot of different clubs at the university.

4 ☐ Richard practises with the orchestra every afternoon.

Listening

Multiple choice

3 **a** Look at the pictures and do the tasks in italics.

1 *Describe the men in the pictures.*

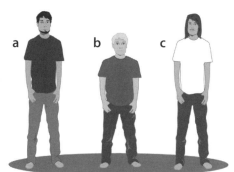

a b c

_____
_____
_____

Which picture shows John?

2 *Name the things in the pictures.*

a b c

_____
_____
_____

What do the women buy?

3 *Write the times using words.*

_____

_____

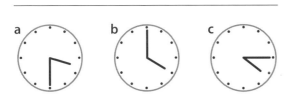

a

b

c

What time do Zoe and Dave agree to meet?

b ⟨5⟩ Now listen and answer the exam questions in exercise 3a.

Use of English
Gap fill

4 Match a word from column A with a word from column B to make collocations.

A	B
1 a packet	a centre
2 sports	b swimming
3 car	c gymnastics
4 do	d lunch
5 go	e of tissues
6 have	f to music
7 listen	g park

5 Read about Anna's typical Saturday. Complete the text with the words below. There is one extra word that you do not need.

> centre   do   go   have   home   often
> packet   play   park   to   up ✓

Anna's Saturday

On Saturdays I'm very active. I get ¹ *up* at eight o'clock. I go to the sports ² _____ . I've got a big bag with my clothes, my equipment, a big bottle of water and a ³ _____ of tissues. I meet my friends in the car ⁴ _____ at the centre. We ⁵ _____ gymnastics for an hour and then we ⁶ _____ swimming. After that we ⁷ _____ lunch in a café and then we go ⁸ _____ and relax. Sometimes we listen ⁹ _____ music, sometimes we watch a film. In the evening we ¹⁰ _____ go dancing.

Speaking
Talking about yourself

6 Tick (✓) the best answer.

Examiner: *Have you got any brothers and sisters?*

Student:

a ☐ *Yes.*

b ☐ *Yes, I've got two sisters. Eva is twenty and Jana is fourteen. Eva studies Physics at university. We're very good friends.*

7 Match questions 1–5 to answers a–e.

1 Tell me about your family.
2 Have you got a best friend?
3 What sports do you like?
4 What do you usually do at weekends?
5 What do you like about your city or town?

a I like my town because there's a lot to do.
b I live with my mother, father and my little sister Barbara.
c I read or I do sports.
d Oh, all kinds, really. I like swimming, running, tennis, skiing, football, basketball.
e Yes, I have. His name is Kristof.

8 Add sentences 1–5 below to answers a–f in exercise 7 to add more information.

1 He's not very tall but very good at sports. We do a lot of sports together. And he is a very good friend. When I have a problem, he always listens to me. ___

2 I go surfing every summer and skiing every winter. I also do karate. ___

3 My brother Marko doesn't live with us, he's studying in Germany. But we all meet in the holidays. ___

4 There are some good cinemas and a very good new sports centre with a swimming pool. And there's a really nice park in the centre. ___

5 These are my two favourite activities, so every weekend I read a bit at home and then I go out and play sports with my friends. I also go to the cinema a lot. ___

exam trainer 1

self-assessment test 2

Vocabulary & Grammar

1 Choose the best word or expression a, b or c to complete the sentences.

1 Our new kitchen is great. We've got a new cooker and a new
   a armchair. **b** fridge. ✓ **c** sofa.

2 You can buy bread at the
   a greengrocer's. **b** baker's.
   c newsagent's.

3 My two sisters sleep upstairs. They've got a big
   a bedroom. **b** living room.
   c bathroom.

4 Is your shoe size seven? You've got very big
   a arms. **b** feet. **c** legs.

5 Your new T-shirt? I think it's in the ___ in your room.
   a sink **b** bookcase **c** wardrobe

6 I can't walk. I've got
   a a cough. **b** an earache.
   c a pain in my knee.

7 There are a lot of cars in my city. The traffic is
   a terrible. **b** polluted. **c** exciting.

8 We use a rope for
   a rowing. **b** skiing. **c** rock climbing.

9 Robert ___ judo twice a week.
   a goes **b** does **c** plays

/8

2 Complete the sentences with one word in each gap.

1 We've got a new washing _machine_ .

2 It hurts when I talk. I've got a _____ throat.

3 I swim three times a week in a local swimming _____ .

4 A _____ shop sells pens and paper.

5 My grandmother is very ill. She's in _____ and we visit her every day.

6 People have ten fingers and ten _____ .

7 Do you live in a house or in a _____ ?

8 Do you sometimes _____ skiing in winter?

/7

3 Some of these sentences are wrong. Tick (✓) the correct sentences or cross (✗) the wrong ones.

1 How much money have you got?
   ✓

2 Is there some post office near your school?
   Is there a post office near your school?

3 How many girls are there in your class?
   _____

4 Do you eat much apples?
   _____

5 I haven't got a space on my desk.
   _____

6 Are there some sports centres in your town?
   _____

7 There is a lot of milk in the fridge.
   _____

/5

4 Complete the conversation with *can* or *can't* and the verb in brackets.

A: ¹ _Can you play_ (you/play) basketball, Bethany?

B: No, I ² _____ . I hate team sports. And you?

A: I ³ _____ (play) it but not very well. My brother is brilliant at it. He's good at all sports. He ⁴ _____ (do) karate and gymnastics.

B: Really? ⁵ _____ (he/swim) well, too?

A: Yes, he ⁶ _____ . He's the best swimmer in our school.

/5

5 <u>Underline</u> the correct words to complete the sentences.

1 My sister can speak French very *good/well*.

2 He walks *slow/slowly* because he's got a sore leg.

3 You haven't got much money? *You find/Find* a part time job.

4 Robert is a *good/well* volleyball player.

5 *Don't watch/Not watch* TV now – you've got a lot of homework.

6 I can't understand him – he speaks very *quick/quickly*.

/5

38

Listening

6 (6) Listen to the conversation between Scott Perkins and a young sportswoman. Choose the correct answer a, b or c.

1 Scott is at
   a school.   b the sports centre.
   c the university.

2 Kate's team usually play basketball
   a twice a week.   b three times a week.
   c every day.

3 Kate is also a good
   a volleyball player.   b surfer.
   c swimmer.

4 Kate sometimes does shopping in
   a a music shop.   b a bookstore.
   c a shopping mall.

5 At the end of the conversation Kate
   a has got backache.   b feels sick.
   c has got a pain in her knee.

/5

Communication

7 Write a question for the answers with the words in brackets.

1 _What sports do you watch on TV?_
   (what/watch/TV)
   I watch football and gymnastics.

2 _____ ?
   (do/any sports)
   Yes, I go swimming and play tennis.

3 _____ ?
   (be/your city/famous)
   Oh, yes it is! Everyone knows Paris.

4 _____ ?
   (shops/good/in your town)
   Yes, we've got two big shopping malls.

5 _____ ?
   (what/favourite)
   Basketball and skiing.

/4

8 Underline the correct words in the dialogue.

Peter: [1] _Excuse_/Sorry me. How do I [2] go/get to the town hall from here?

Woman: Let me see. You [3] take/turn left into West Street. Then you [4] take/turn the second right into Pine Road. The town hall's on the left. You [5] don't/can't miss it!

Peter: [6] Thank/Thanks you very much.

/5

Reading

9 Read the email from Ella to Alexia. Tick (✓) true or cross (✗) false.

To: Alexia@gmail98.com
From: Ella@tgmail67.com
Subject: Hello from Ireland!

Hi Alexia,

Hello from Ireland! Yes, I am in Ireland now. My dad has got a new job and we've got a new house here. It's fantastic! And it's quite big – there are three bedrooms (my parents', my sister's and mine), a living room, a kitchen and a bathroom. My bedroom is small but I like it a lot and I spend a lot of time here. I've got a new bookcase and an armchair so I often sit and read my books and magazines. And I play computer games or chat on the Internet.

My sister's bedroom is really big, maybe because she's only got a bed and a small wardrobe in it. She hasn't got a computer or a bookcase. And she's never home. I think she's got a new boyfriend!

My new school is OK and I've got two new friends. We often go to a shopping mall after school. We don't go into the shops, we just meet there and hang out with some other friends. Or we sometimes play volleyball in a local park. My new town is quite small but I like it a lot. There's only one problem – there's a lot of traffic here. But buses are good so I always get to school on time.

I hope you're well.

Love,
Ella

1 ☐ Ella likes her new house.
2 ☐ Ella has got a lot of space in her bedroom.
3 ☐ There is a computer in Ella's bedroom.
4 ☐ Ella's sister hasn't got much furniture in her bedroom.
5 ☐ Ella often goes shopping after school.
6 ☐ Ella walks to school.

/6

Marks

Vocabulary & Grammar	/30 marks
Listening	/5 marks
Communication	/9 marks
Reading	/6 marks
Total:	/50 marks

Vocabulary

Food

1 Label the food pictures.

1 _a_ p p l _e_ s

2 _ _ _ _ _ a s

3 e _ _ s

4 _ i _ _

5 _ _ _ c _ i _ s

6 c _ _ _ p s

2 Put the words from exercise 1 in the correct column.

healthy	unhealthy
apples	

3 Complete the sentences with the words below.

vegetables   milk ✓   salad   junk
drink   potatoes

1 Do you often drink _milk_ ?
2 _____ are vegetables.
3 Robert often makes a _____ with tomatoes, rice and vegetables.
4 Are you tired? Take some exercise and don't eat _____ food!
5 Keith and Tom never _____ fruit juice.
6 Susanna always buys fresh _____ at the market.

Grammar

like/love/hate + ing

4 (*) Complete the sentences with the _-ing_ form of the verb in brackets.

1 They love _making_ pizzas. (make)
2 Elsa hates _____ tea. (drink)
3 We love _____ CDs. (buy)
4 Liz hates _____ tennis. (play)
5 Ali loves _____ ice-cream. (eat)
6 Mario likes _____ pasta. (cook)

5 (**) Make the sentences negative.

1 Mark likes eating salad.
   Mark doesn't like eating salad.
2 Tim and Beth like playing video games.
   _____
3 Harry likes eating onions.
   _____
4 Linda likes doing Maths homework.
   _____
5 Jerry likes drinking coffee.
   _____
6 Paul and Sue like going for a walk.
   _____

6 (**) Put the words in the correct order to make questions. Then answer the questions.

1 pizzas/Do/like/you/making
   Do you like making pizzas?
2 your sister/reading/Does/like
   _____ ?
3 football/playing/Do/your friends/like
   _____ ?
4 music/Do/listening/you/to/like
   _____ ?
5 your family/like/food/junk/eating/Does
   _____ ?
6 hate/Do/you/studying/Maths
   _____ ?

7 ⚫⚫ Write sentences with *love* (☺☺), *like* (☺) and *hate* (☹).

1 Chris ☺☺ drink coffee/☹ drink tea.

   Chris loves drinking coffee but he
   hates drinking tea.

2 My parents ☺ listen music/☹ watch TV

   _____

   _____ .

3 My friends ☹ do homework/☺ go to the cinema

   _____

   _____ .

4 Carla ☺ cook/☹ wash up

   _____

   _____ .

5 Belinda ☺☺ read books/☹ watch films

   _____

   _____ .

6 Marco ☺ eat healthy food/☺☺ do exercise

   _____

   _____ .

7 Jane ☹ play tennis/☺ do gymnastics

   _____

   _____ .

8 Ben ☺☺ play football/ ☹ do karate

   _____

   _____ .

8 ⚫ Read the questions and write short answers. Use the information in exercise 7.

1 Does Chris like drinking coffee?

   Yes, he does.

2 Do your parents like watching TV?

   _____ .

3 Do your friends like going to the cinema?

   _____ .

4 Does Carla like cooking?

   _____ .

5 Does Belinda love reading books?

   _____ .

6 Does Marco like eating healthy food?

   _____ .

7 Does Jane like doing gymnastics?

   _____ .

8 Does Ben hate playing football?

   _____ .

Grammar reference

like/love/hate + ing

After *love*, *like*, *hate* and *prefer* we use the *-ing* form.

My little sister **loves going** to school.
Do you **like cycling**?
I **hate getting up** early on Sundays.

Form

+	I/You/We/They **like eating** He/She/It **likes eating**	ice-cream.
−	I/You/We/They **don't like eating** He/She/It **doesn't like eating**	
?	**Do** I/you/we/they **like eating** **Does** has he/she/it like eating	ice-cream?

Short answers	Yes, I/you/we/they **do**. No, I/you/we/they **don't**. Yes, he/she/it **does**. No, he/she/it **doesn't**.

Wh- questions	Answers
Why *does she hate swimming?*	*Because she's doesn't like water.*
What *do you like cooking?*	*Italian food.*

Vocabulary

Cooking

1 Complete the sentences with the words below.

> boil   lemon   Tuna ✓   cake   bean
> vegetarian

1 _Tuna_ is a type of fish.
2 Do you know how to _____ an egg?
3 A _____ doesn't eat meat or fish.
4 A green _____ is a healthy vegetable.
5 A _____ is a yellow fruit.
6 Dan likes eating _____ and biscuits.
  He doesn't like healthy food!

2 Complete the recipe with the words below.

> Put (x2)   Mix (x2)   Cut ✓   Cook

1 _Cut_ the potatoes and onions into
  small pieces.
2 _____ some olive oil into a frying pan.

3 _____ the potatoes and onions
  together and put them into the frying pan.
4 _____ the eggs.
5 _____ the eggs in the frying pan with
  the potatoes and onions.
6 _____ for 5–10 minutes.

Grammar

Articles

3 ⊛ Put the food words in the correct column.

> milk   crisps   rice   fish   onion   juice
> cheese   meat   apple   egg   cereal
> pizza   tomato   potato   ice-cream
> biscuit ✓   coffee

countable	uncountable
biscuit	

4 ⊛ Complete the sentences with *a* or *an*.
1 My sister's husband is _a_ chef.
2 ___ tomato is a red vegetable.
3 You've got a cold? Eat ___ orange every day.
4 Cake and ice-cream is ___ unhealthy snack.
5 ___ apple is a healthy food.
6 Let's have ___ pizza for lunch.
7 My brother is ___ vegetarian.
8 I have ___ egg for breakfast.

5 ⊛ Complete the sentences with *a*, *an* or *the*.
1 There is _a_ new cinema in my town.
  The cinema is near my house.
2 Cut ___ tomato into pieces. Put ___ pieces
  in ___ sandwich.
3 Boil ___ egg in some water for three
  minutes. Carefully, take ___ egg out of ___
  boiling water.
4 ___ onion is ___ type of vegetable.
5 ___ homework for tonight is ___ grammar
  exercise on page 10.
6 I've got ___ great birthday present for my
  brother. It's ___ camera.

6 (✱✱) Michelle is at a cooking school in London. Complete her postcard with *a*, *an*, *the* or ø (no article).

Hi Mum,

Here I am, at ¹ ___ cooking school in ² ___ London. It's great here! I live near the centre and I usually walk to lessons because ³ ___ traffic is very bad in ⁴ ___ city centre.

There are four hours of lessons a day! ⁵ ___ lessons are really fun but also hard work. Today's lesson is how to cook ⁶ ___ Italian food – great! I love ⁷ ___ pasta!

See you soon!

Michelle

London, England

Grammar Plus: Article or no article

7 (✱✱) Complete the sentences with *a*, *an*, *the* or ø (no article).

1 Barack Obama is ___ famous man. He is ___ president of ___ USA.
2 Sydney is ___ big city in Australia. It isn't ___ capital of Australia. ___ capital is Canberra.
3 Manchester City are ___ famous British football team. Their stadium is in ___ Manchester.
4 Get ___ tomato. Cut ___ tomato into four pieces.
5 I love listening to ___ Indian music. I love ___ music in Indian films.
6 I eat ___ lot of fruit and vegetables because I'm ___ vegetarian.

Grammar reference

Articles *a/an/the*

a/an

We use *a/an* in the following ways:

• with countable singular nouns. We use *a* before words beginning with a consonant and *an* before words beginning with a vowel.

a **h**ouse, *a* **d**og
an **a**pple, *an* **e**gg

• when we mention a thing or a person for the first time.

*I've got **a** cat and **a** dog.*
*There is **a** desk in my room.*

• to describe a thing or a person with the verb *to be*.

*Julia Roberts is **an** actress.*
*Are you **a** vegetarian?*

the

We use *the* in the following ways.

• with singular and plural nouns when we talk about a thing or a person again.

*I've got a cat and a dog. **The** dog is very big.*

• when we talk about a specific thing and our listener knows which one we mean.

*Where is **the** cat?* (I've got only one cat)
***The** girls in my class are very nice.* (these ones in my class)

• with musical instruments.

*My sister plays **the** piano.*

No article (ø)

We don't use articles when:

• we generalise.

I don't like pizza. (pizza in general)
Robert loves tomatoes. (tomatoes in general)

• with sports, activities and school subjects.

He plays football very well.
We often go swimming.
I don't like Maths.

• with the names of places.

My grandparents live in Warsaw.

• with most countries.

They come from Sweden.
What's the capital of Italy?

> **Notice!**
>
> *Barbara lives in England.*
> *Barbara lives in **the** United Kingdom.*
>
> *They're going to America.*
> *They're going to **the** USA.*

Vocabulary

Food

1 Complete the sentences with the words below.

> meal   breakfast   foreign food ✓   lunch
> traditional dish   ready meals   dessert

1 My mum loves _foreign food_ , especially Indian and Chinese.

2 Judy always has _____ before she goes to school.

3 Fish and chips is a _____ in Britain.

4 Supermarkets sell a lot of _____ for people who haven't got much time.

5 At school the _____ break is from 12.30 to 1.30.

6 On my birthday I go to a special restaurant for my favourite _____ : lasagne and chips!

7 The children's favourite _____ is ice-cream.

2 Look at the pictures and write when you have each food or drink: breakfast, lunch or dessert

1 _breakfast_

2 _____

3 _____

4 _____

6 _____

5 _____

7 _____

8 _____

Reading

3 Before you read, look at the photo of Vera. Where do you think Vera works? Read the text and check.

1 restaurant   3 café

2 school   4 supermarket

Read about Vera. She has a very important job, she is a dinner lady at St Alban's school in Swindon.

1 ☐

I love my job. I like working with young people and I love preparing food. I cook lunch every day in the school canteen and I also help to serve the food. Then I clean up – I suppose I am a waitress, chef and cleaner! I work with seven other dinner ladies because there are around 1,400 students at our school and that is a lot of meals!

2 ☐

My job is sometimes difficult. We try to cook healthy meals and to teach students to eat healthily but some students don't always listen. They sometimes say they don't like the food. I think it's important that students understand that healthy food is really important.

3 ☐

There isn't any junk food in the school canteen and there aren't any ready meals. We use fresh ingredients

4 Match the headings a–e with the paragraphs 1–5 of the text.

  a Favourite food **d** My job
  b School dinners **e** Problems
  c Snacks

5 Read the text again and tick (✓) true or cross (✗) false.

  1 ☐ Vera does not like her job.
  2 ☐ There are 1,400 students at St Alban's school.
  3 ☐ Not all students love healthy food.
  4 ☐ They sometimes cook junk food at the school.
  5 ☐ In the break students often have fizzy drinks.
  6 ☐ All the students love the idea of free fruit.
  7 ☐ Vera doesn't like pizza.

6 Answer the questions.

  1 How many dinner ladies are there at St Alban's school.

  _____

  2 What kind of food does Vera cook in the school canteen?

  _____

  3 What does Vera think is the perfect healthy meal?

  _____

  4 What do students often eat at break?

  _____

  5 How much do the students pay for fruit at break?

  _____

  6 Why doesn't Vera want the students to know what her favourite dessert is?

  _____

or all our meals. We sometimes cook traditional British food but we often have foreign food especially Italian or Chinese. I think the perfect healthy meal is meat or fish with vegetables and rice or potatoes and fresh fruit for dessert.

☐

the break students often eat crisps or chocolate and zzy drinks, so now we give the students free fruit and ilk so they can have a healthy snack. This is a very popular ea, parents love it and some students love it, too!

☐

think that a lot of students' favourite meal is pizza, and e-cream for dessert. I like that, too but you can't eat it very day. My favourite meal is lasagne and salad and my ourite dessert is chocolate cake but don't tell the udents!

Listening

7 (7) Listen to the coversation and tick (✓) the food that the students talk about.

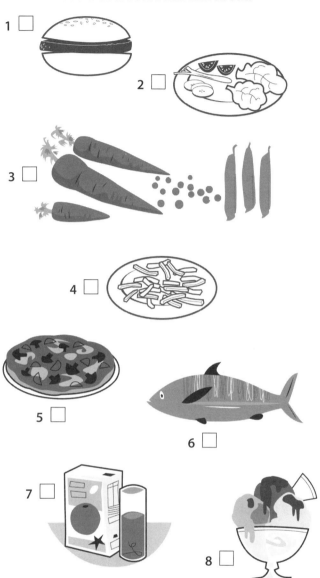

1 ☐
2 ☐
3 ☐
4 ☐
5 ☐
6 ☐
7 ☐
8 ☐

8 (7) Listen again and say if the students like (✓), love (✓✓), don't like (✗) or hate (✗✗) the food.

Name	Dave	Linda	Macy
burger			
fish and chips			
vegetables			
salad			

9 (8) Listen to part 2 and tick (✓) true or cross (✗) false.

  1 ☐ Macy has rice and meat for dinner.
  2 ☐ There are no chips today.
  3 ☐ There is pizza today.
  4 ☐ Dave doesn't want pasta or vegetables.
  5 ☐ Linda has a chicken sandwich.
  6 ☐ Linda doesn't want any salad.

Writing

A postcard

> Dear Bill,
>
> I hope you are well.
>
> I'm here in London with my mum and dad. We're in a very interesting art gallery. It's called the Tate.
>
> This is a fantastic city for art and culture and there are lots of museums. I think my favourite is the Science Museum. There are lots of cafés and fantastic restaurants, and you can find every kind of shop. It's a brilliant city but it is quite polluted.
>
> See you soon.
>
> Lots of love,
> Angela

1 Begin the post card with *Hi* or *Dear* + name of person: *Dear Mum, Hi Gerry,*

2 Say where you are: *I'm in London, I'm in a great café.*

3 Give information about the place/ your holiday: *This is a brilliant city. It's a brilliant city.*

> 57 Rynek Starego Miasta,
> 00-272 Warsaw,
> Poland

4 End the postcard: *See you soon.*

5 Sign off and write your name: *Lots of love, Joan*

1 Read the postcard and <u>underline</u> the correct words.

1 Angela is in *Madrid/London*.

2 She is with *her mum and dad/Bill*.

3 They are in a *museum/gallery*.

4 There are lots of *galleries/restaurants*.

5 Her favourite museum is the *Science Museum/the Tate*.

2 Complete the postcard with the phrases below.

> There are lots of museums,   It's called the Boboli Garden.
> My favourite gallery   I hope you are OK. ✓
> See you soon.   The city has got some very nice cafés.

> Dear Mum,
>
> ¹ <u>I hope you are OK.</u>
>
> I'm here in Florence with my classmates. We're in a wonderful garden.
> ² _____ It's very beautiful.
>
> This is a fantastic city for art and culture.
> ³ _____ galleries and famous buildings. ⁴ _____ is the Uffizi. There are lots of famous paintings.
> ⁵ _____ There are lots of nice restaurants, too but it is very expensive.
>
> ⁶ _____
>
> Lots of love,
> Terry

3 We can use *and* to give more information and *but* to contrast information. <u>Underline</u> examples of *and* and *but* in Angela and Terry's postcards.

4 Match phrases 1–5 with phrases a–e to make sentences.

1 There are lots of galleries

2 The teachers are nice

3 The beach is beautiful

4 There are lots of cafés

5 It's an exciting city

a but there aren't many restaurants.

b and museums.

c and the students are friendly.

d but it is very polluted.

e but the sea is cold.

5 Complete the postcard with the adjectives and linkers below. Use each adjective once.

> new ✓ friendly polluted beautiful
> but terrible exciting and (x2)
> great delicious

Hi Dad,

I hope you're well.

I'm in Brighton in my ¹ _new_ school. There are lots of ² _____ students in the school. Brighton has got a ³ _____ beach, ⁴ _____ the weather here is ⁵ _____ . It's very rainy. There are lots of ⁶ _____ restaurants ⁷ _____ the food here is ⁸ _____ . There are lots of tourists here ⁹ _____ there is lots of traffic, too. Brighton is ¹⁰ _____ but there is a lot to see and do here — it is a very ¹¹ _____ city.

Lots of love,
Will

6 Complete the strategies box with the words below.

> where End information Hi ✓

Writing a postcard

• Greet the person you are writing to: ¹ _Hi_ , Dear + name

• Say ² _____ you are and who you are with: I'm here in Seville./I'm here with Jo.

• Give ³ _____ about the place. Use adjectives to describe it: This is a brilliant city.

• ⁴ _____ you postcard: Lots of love, Terry

7 Read the task and then write your postcard. Use the strategies in exercise 6 to help you.

> You are on holiday with your friends in England. Write a postcard to your English class.
> • Say where you are.
> • Say who you are with.
> • Describe the place.

Speaking

Ordering food and drink

8 Put the phrases in the correct order to complete the dialogue.

Waiter: help/can/you/I
¹ _Can I help you?_

Tim: I'd like a burger, please.

Waiter: to/OK/and/drink?
² _____ .

Tim: Water, please.

Waiter: Anything else?

Tim: have/a/salad/can/please/I?
³ _____ .

Waiter: OK, that's £5.40, please.

Tim: you/here/are
⁴ _____ .

Waiter: your/here's/change
⁵ _____ .

Tim: Thanks.

9 Complete the dialogue with the phrases below.

> How much is that   A fruit juice
> What would you like ✓   Here you are
> Anything else   I'd like salad, please

Waiter: ¹ _What would you like?_

Luke: Can I have a cheese sandwich, please?

Waiter: And to drink?

Luke: ² _____ , please.

Waiter: ³ _____ ?

Luke: ⁴ _____ .

Waiter: OK, so a cheese sandwich, a fruit juice and a salad.

Luke: ⁵ _____ ?

Waiter: That's £4.10, please.

Luke: ⁶ _____ ?

Waiter: Here's your change.

6 my time

* easy to do
** a bit harder

Vocabulary

Free time

1 Label the activities.

> have dinner   babysit ✓   watch a film
> have a piano lesson

1 _babysit_

2 _____

3 _____

4 _____

2 Rearrange the letters in the words to complete the sentences.

1 Do you **mkae** _make_ a lot of phonecalls on your mobile?

2 I usually **pehl** _____ my parents at the weekend.

3 My friend Bruno comes to my house and we **kwro** _____ on school projects.

4 My sister has got my computer. She wants to **aolddnwo** _____ some music.

5 After school I often hang out at the mall and **hatc** _____ with friends.

3 Complete the sentences with the words below.

> email ✓   music   games   dinner
> project

1 Alana is writing an _email_ to her friend.

2 Serena is working on a school _____ on the computer.

3 I often download _____ from the Internet.

4 My brother loves playing computer _____ .

5 We're having _____ with our friends at the moment.

Grammar

Present continuous

4 (*) Complete the postcard with the correct form of the verbs in brackets.

Dear Mum and Dad,

Jill and I ¹ _are having_ (have) a great time in Edinburgh! The weather is great, the shops are fantastic and the people are nice. At the moment, I ² _____ (sit) in a café and I ³ _____ (eat) fish and chips. I ⁴ _____ (read) about Edinburgh castle – I really want to go there!

Jill likes Edinburgh too. She isn't here now, she ⁵ _____ (visit) the Museum of Edinburgh and ⁶ _____ (learn) about Scottish history.

See you soon!

Kate xx

5 (**) Look at the picture. Write what the people are doing.

1 Mark _is texting his friend_ .

2 Liz _____ .

3 Matt _____ .

4 Lisa _____ .

48

6 (✷✷) **Look at the picture on page 48 again. Then write questions and answer them.**

1 Mark/eat lunch?

   Is Mark eating lunch?

   No, he isn't. He's texting.

2 Matt and Lisa/have lunch?

   _____

   _____

3 Liz/do a project?

   _____

   _____

4 Liz and Mark/chatting?

   _____

   _____

5 Lisa/listen to music?

   _____

   _____

7 (✷✷) **Put the words in the correct order to make sentences.**

1 today/mother/working/your/is

   Is your mother working today?

2 History/aren't/today/studying/we

   _____ .

3 isn't/the/moving/train

   _____ .

4 uniform/wearing/I'm/today/not/school

   _____ .

5 music/downloading/we're/some

   _____ .

6 homework/doing/are/they/their

   _____ ?

Grammar Plus: Present continuous: spelling rules

8 (✷✷) **Complete the dialogue with the correct form of the verbs in brackets.**

Bill: Hi Liz! Where are you?

Liz: I'm in my aunt's flat.

Bill: What ¹_____ you _____ (do)?

Liz: I ²_____ (work) on a school project. I ³_____ (get) some information from the Internet. What ⁴_____ you _____ (do)?

Bill: I ⁵_____ (hang out) with Ben, we ⁶_____ (shop) at the shopping mall. Do you want to see a film?

Liz : Sorry, I'm busy.

Bill: *Star Wars* is at the Rex Cinema. Come and join me.

Liz: I'm sorry. I can't. I ⁷_____ (babysit) for my niece and we ⁸_____ (make) pizza.

Bill: OK. See you at school tomorrow. Bye!

Liz: Bye, Bill.

Grammar reference

Present continuous

Form

+	I *am* (*'m*) *reading* You/We/They *are* (*'re*) *reading* He/She/It *is* (*'s*) *reading*	
–	I *am not* (*'m not*) *reading* You/We/They *are not* (*aren't*) *reading* He/She/It *is not* (*isn't*) *reading*	a book now.
?	*Am* I *reading* *Are* you/we/they *reading* *Is* he/she/it *reading*	a book now?

Short answers	Yes, I *am*. No, I'*m not*. Yes, you/we/they *are*. No, you/we/they *aren't*. Yes, he/she/it *is*. No, he/she/it *isn't*.

Wh- questions	Answers
Where are you going? *What* are you doing? *Why* is Jane surfing the net?	I'm going to school. I'm watching TV. Because she is working on a school project.

Use

We use the present continuous to talk about actions happening at the moment of speaking.

I'*m watching* 'Friends' on TV now.
They *aren't dancing*.
Is Ann *doing* her homework now? No, she *isn't*.

Spelling of the *-ing* form

With verbs ending in a single vowel *-e*, we omit *-e* in the *-ing* form:

give → giving, *have → having*, *come → coming*

With verbs ending in a single consonant after a single vowel, we often double the final consonant.

sit → sitting, *chat → chatting*, *run → running*

Vocabulary

Clothes

1 Label the types of clothes.

1 s _kirt_   2 j _ _ _ _ t   3 s _ _ _ f   4 h _ t

6 b _ _ t

5 d _ _ _ s   7 t _ _ _ _ _ s   8 h _ _ _ e

2 Complete the sentences with the words below.

> piercing   T-shirts   trainers   hat ✓
> shirt   dress   shoes

1 I usually wear a _hat_ on cold days in the winter.

2 Harry's school uniform is a white _____ and blue trousers.

3 My sister's school uniform is a brown _____ and black _____ .

4 Mandy has got a _____ in her nose.

5 I wear _____ and a T-shirt to do sport.

6 They are going to watch their local football team so they are wearing red and white _____ .

Grammar

Present simple and present continuous

3 (✱) <u>Underline</u> the correct form to complete the sentences.

1 I often _hang out/am hanging out_ with my friends on Saturdays.

2 She _wears/is wearing_ a hoodie and jeans today.

3 He _goes/is going_ to school by bus every day.

4 My dad _reads/is reading_ the newspaper now.

5 We _download/are downloading_ music at the moment.

6 They _have/are having_ dinner in a restaurant twice a week.

4 (✱) Match the questions 1–6 with the answers a–f.

1 What do you wear at school?

2 What are you wearing at the moment?

3 What's Susanna doing now?

4 What time does Ben usually go to bed.

5 What are Steve and Sarah doing now?

6 When do you usually have dinner?

a She's downloading music.

b They're playing tennis.

c I wear school uniform.

d I usually have dinner at seven o'clock.

e I'm wearing a T-shirt and jeans.

f He usually goes to bed at ten o'clock.

5 (✱✱) Rewrite the sentences using the word in brackets.

1 Kit is wearing trainers now. (every day)
   Kit wears trainers every day.

2 David usually wears his school uniform. (today)
   David is wearing his school uniform today.

3 My friends are wearing casual clothes today. (often)

_____

4 Sometimes I wear a lot of jewellery. (now)

_____

5 Bethany makes a salad every day. (at the moment)

_____

6 We're cooking dinner at the moment. (every day)

_____

6 (**) Complete the text with the correct form of the verb in brackets.

Polly usually ¹ _goes_ (go) shopping on Friday, but today she ² _____ (have) dinner at her uncle and aunt's house in Spain. They ³ _____ (eat) a special Spanish dinner. Polly ⁴ _____ (sit) near her uncle. She ⁵ _____ (talk) to him.

Polly's uncle and aunt usually ⁶ _____ (have) a big dinner every Friday. Her aunt ⁷ _____ (be) a good cook and she always ⁸ _____ (make) nice food. Her uncle and aunt usually ⁹ _____ (speak) Spanish but tonight they ¹⁰ _____ (speak) in English.

7 (**) Put the words in the correct order to make sentences.

1 aren't/History/studying/they/today
  They aren't studying History today.

2 music/what/listening to/are/you
  _____ ?

3 school/at/study/they/French
  _____ .

4 today/they/wearing/aren't/school uniform
  _____ .

5 does/work/Mr Davis/in/your school
  _____ ?

6 are/film/they/at the moment/what/watching
  _____ ?

Grammar reference

Present simple and present continuous

Present simple

We use the present simple to talk about habits/routines or facts/things that are generally true.

*I usually **go** to sleep at ten o'clock.* (habit/routine)
*Matthew **doesn't like** mushrooms.* (fact)

We often use the present simple with these adverbs of frequency:
always, usually, often, sometimes, never, every day/week/month, once/twice a week, three/four/ten times a year.

*I **often wear** this skirt.*
*She **never eats** meat.*
*They **go** to Spain **once a year**.*

Present continuous

We use the present continuous to talk about actions happening at the moment of speaking.

I'm tired – I'm going to bed.
(action happening at the moment of speaking)

We often use the present continuous with these adverbs of frequency:
now, right now, at the moment, today.

*She's **talking** to Sandra **at the moment**.*
*I'm **not wearing** my favourite earrings **today**.*
*What **is** Robert **doing now**?*

> **Notice!**
>
> We can use the present simple and present continuous in the same sentence.
>
> *We often **have** pasta for dinner but today we're **having** fish and chips.*

Vocabulary

The Internet

1 Rearrange the letters to make computer words.

1 hact   _chat_
2 elima   _____
3 glob   _____
4 woaldndo   _____
5 neonli   _____
6 pssawrod   _____

2 Match the words 1–8 with the definitions a–h.

1 password
2 username
3 chat room
4 online
5 email
6 web page
7 download
8 log on

a a place on the Internet to chat and make friends
b a message you send on the Internet
c getting music and games from the Internet
d the name you use on the Internet
e when you are connected to the Internet.
f a page on the Internet
g you type your username and password to do this
h a secret word you use to log on to websites

3 Complete the sentences with the words below.

> chat   web page   password ✓   online
> download   email

1 I don't use my real name in my _password_ .
2 Mike sends me an _____ every day.
3 I use the Internet to _____ games and photos.
4 Sue can _____ to her friends for hours on the Internet.
5 The class has its own _____ with all our profiles on it.
6 You need to be _____ to send an email.

Reading

4 Look at the reading text. What type of text is it?

a a newspaper article   b a web page
c an email

5 Read the article. Match the phrases a–f with the gaps 1–6.

a I think that adults need to socialise more, not teenagers.
b Is this really true?
c I agree with Betsy.
d are teenagers spending too much time online?
e There are so many things you can do on your computer.
f We text and chat and send messages.

6 Read the article again. Tick (✓) true or cross (✗) false.

1 ☐ Adults think using computers too much is unhealthy.
2 ☐ Adults think teenagers don't spend time in the real world.
3 ☐ Lily has got a computer.
4 ☐ Lily uses her computer for seven hours each day.
5 ☐ Betsy only communicates using the Internet.
6 ☐ Betsy uses the Internet at least once a day.
7 ☐ Jaz is Betsy's friend.
8 ☐ Bob doesn't use the Internet to chat to friends.

BlogSpeakOut

| HOME | BROWSE | DISCUSSION | FORUMS | BLOGS |

On this week's discussion board we ask – **1** _d_ .
A lot of adults think that teenagers use their computers too much and that this is not healthy. They think that teenagers spend too much time online, visiting sites like Bebo and MySpace and that they don't spend time in the real world talking to people and making real friends. **2** ___ What do you think?

But that's not true! I don't spend a lot of time online but I do use my computer. I also spend a lot of time at school. I think that adults forget that teenagers are with other people for seven hours or more every day. We are with our classmates, talking to each other! **3** ___
Lily, 15

I use the Internet to chat to my friends. **4** ___ I think this is very sociable. I communicate a lot. In fact I create blog pages so I can tell my friends what I am doing all the time and upload photographs. I write my news on there once

7 Choose the correct answer.

1 Many adults
   a think that teenagers use the Internet too much.
   b think that adults use the Internet too much.
   c think that teenagers are unhealthy.

2 Lily doesn't spend
   a a lot of time on the Internet.
   b a lot of time at school.
   c a lot of time with her class mates.

3 Lily thinks adults
   a need to spend more time at school.
   b need to spend more time socialising.
   c need to spend more time on the Internet.

4 Betsy
   a writes news on her blog everyday.
   b uploads photographs everyday.
   c phones her friends every day.

5 Jaz
   a has got a lot of friends at school.
   b has got a lot of friends on the Internet.
   c hasn't got a lot of friends at school.

6 Bob uses the Internet for
   a uploading photos and chatting to friends.
   b talking to friends.
   c doing homework and chatting to friends.

Log in   Register   SEARCH Computers and teenagers

a day, sometimes more. I have a lot of friends and I write messages to them, and I text and phone a lot, too. I think I am a very, very sociable person.
Betsy, 15

Yeah, **5** ___ But I think she is lucky that she has so many friends. I am really shy and I don't have a lot of friends at school. I think the Internet is a great way to chat and make new friends. It's a very positive experience for a lot of teenagers.
Jaz, 14

Computers are useful for so many things. I don't just use the Internet to chat to friends, I watch videos, download music, share games with friends, I also use it for homework. **6** ___ I think that it is normal to spend a lot of time in front of a computer.
Bob, 16

Listening

8 (9) Listen to part 1 of the radio interview. Tick (✓) true or cross (✗) false.

1 ☐ Most teenagers chat on the Internet to people they already know.
2 ☐ It is normal to receive emails from people you do not know on the Internet.
3 ☐ Teenage girls use the Internet more than teenage boys.
4 ☐ Girls use the Internet to make new friends.
5 ☐ Carol thinks chatting to friends on the Internet is normal.
6 ☐ Carol uses the Internet more than most teenagers.

9 (9) Listen again. Match the numbers 1–5 with sentences a–e from the interview.

1 55%   a Twenty-two percent go online more than once a day.

2 70%   b I spend about four hours on the Internet a day!

3 22%   c Most teenagers spend about two hours online a day.

4 Two   d Seventy percent of 15–17-year-old girls have profile pages.

5 Four   e Fifty-five percent of teenagers have profile pages.

10 (10) Listen to part 2. Who says the sentences below: Gerry, Alice or Mike.

1 'I know where my son is and what he is doing.'   *Gerry*

2 'He doesn't spend much time with other people.'   _____

3 'When we are eating, she is texting.'   _____

4 'He is helping me learn about computers now too.'   _____

5 'She's always on the Internet.'   _____

6 'I don't know what my son does on the Internet.'   _____

self-assessment test 3

Vocabulary & Grammar

1 Complete the sentences with one word in each gap.

1 I love Italian food – p_asta_ is my favourite.

2 I drink orange j_____ for breakfast.

3 My brother is a vegetarian, he doesn't eat m_____ .

4 Chinese people eat a lot of r_____ .

5 What do you want on your b_____ : ham or cheese?

6 I love fresh fruit, especially a_____ .

7 Robbie's favourite pizza is cheese and t_____ .

/6

2 Write the names of the clothes and accessories in the picture.

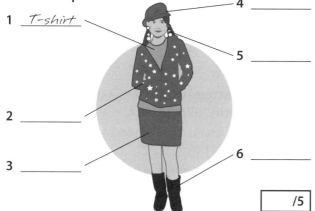

1 _T-shirt_

2 _____

3 _____

4 _____

5 _____

6 _____

/5

3 Write sentences in the present continuous.

1 she/swim/in the sea

   She is swimming in the sea.

2 you/write/a letter?

   _____

3 we/study/history/today

   _____

4 I/not watch/this film

   _____

5 what/he/do?

   _____

6 two students/not listen/to the teacher

   _____

7 where/Tom and Robbie/go?

   _____

/6

4 Choose the best option a, b or c to complete the sentences. Choose ø for no article.

1 I don't really like ___ tomatoes.

   a a   **b** ø ✓   **c** the

2 My brother wants to be ___ actor.

   a a   **b** an   **c** the

3 Can you see a boy and a girl over there? I think ___ girl is very pretty.

   a ø   **b** a   **c** the

4 ___ eggs in the fridge are not fresh – don't eat them!

   a An   **b** The   **c** ø

5 Do you know that ___ carrots are good for your eyes?

   a ø   **b** the   **c** a

6 We've got ___ cat and two rabbits.

   a a   **b** ø   **c** the

7 I never drink ___ milk in the morning.

   a a   **b** the   **c** ø

/6

5 Complete the sentences with the correct form of the verb in brackets. Use the present simple, present continuous, or *like/love/hate* + *ing*.

1 Ann _is talking_ (talk) on her mobile now.

2 I hate _____ (visit) relatives.

3 Stop talking! I _____ (do) my homework.

4 She usually _____ (have) lunch at school.

5 You _____ (wear) a very nice dress today. Is it new?

6 My father _____ (go) to Spain on business three times a year.

7 Mike and Pete are very good at languages. They _____ (speak) English and French.

8 I like _____ (walk) to school. Buses are often late.

/7

Listening

6 (11) Listen to the radio programme.
Tick (✓) true or cross (✗) false.

1 ☐ Amy is wearing a green T-shirt.

2 ☐ Amy has got a lot of stylish friends.

3 ☐ Tim is wearing jeans and a white shirt.

4 ☐ Tim likes wearing his school clothes.

/4

Reading

7 Read the postings page of a website for teenagers. Put sentences a–e in the correct place in the text.

Internet Forum

'Young people eat unhealthy food.' Do you agree? What's your favourite food? And do you think it's good for you? Join our online discussion now!

Cathy

I agree! **1** ___ . I love eating and I eat a lot. I usually have cereal and two pieces of toast in the morning, and then … I'm usually hungry at about ten o'clock at school. **2** ___ . Then I have a sandwich for lunch. And … some biscuits again before dinner. I know it's not very good for you but I do a lot of sport and I'm always hungry.

Samuel

I don't think so! It's not true, certainly not about me! I have a glass of milk in the morning and then my next meal is lunch. I usually make a sandwich for myself. Cheese and tomato is my favourite. I don't often eat meat. **3** ___ . But I'm not because I sometimes eat chicken. I love eggs, they're very quick and easy. My favourite recipe is egg and mushroom omelette. Delicious! **4** ___ .

Debbie

Some people do but not me. My family always eats healthy food. **5** ___ . And I have an apple every day … or grapes – they're my favourite kind of fruit. And I don't eat between meals. I think I can say that I have a very healthy diet.

a Some people think I'm a vegetarian.

b So I have some biscuits or crisps.

c For lunch we usually have meat or fish and a lot of vegetables.

d Most of us don't think about what we eat and drink.

e I often make it for my family and they love it.

/5

Communication

8 Put the sentences in the correct order to make a dialogue.

a ☐ OK, that's £3.50, please.

b ☑1 Can I help you?

c ☐ OK. And to drink?

d ☐ Yes, … . Can I have a ham and tomato sandwich, please? On white bread.

e ☑9 Thanks.

f ☐ I'll have a fruit juice, please.

g ☐ No, thank you.

h ☑8 Here you are.

i ☑5 Anything else?

/5

9 Underline the correct word to complete the dialogues.

1 A: I'm going shopping. How _much_/many is a sandwich?

   B: It's £3.00.

2 A: Do the French usually have toast for breakfast?

   B: I'm not/don't know.

3 A: I think the Italian's favourite lunch is pizza.

   B: I don't agree/sure. I think it's pasta.

4 A: Do you want/can to go to the cinema with me?

   B: Sure.

/3

10 Complete the description of the picture with one word in each gap.

¹ _In_ my picture I can ² _____ a lot of people in the park. ³ _____ the left, three boys are playing football. In the centre, there is a small girl. She's sitting on the grass. ⁴ _____ the background, there are a lot of trees.

/3

Marks

Vocabulary & Grammar	/30 marks
Listening	/4 marks
Reading	/5 marks
Communication	/11 marks
Total:	/50 marks

7 festival fever

* easy to do
** a bit harder

Vocabulary

Music

1 Write in the missing letters to complete the types of music.

1 p _o_ _p_
2 _ _ a s s _ c _ _
3 f o _ _
4 _ e _ v _ m _ _ a _
5 p _ _ k
6 j _ z _
7 _ o _ k
8 _ i - h _ p

2 Complete the sentences with some of the words from exercise 1.

1 Madonna is my favourite _pop_ singer.
2 In the 1980's _____ music was popular in London.
3 The saxophone is a popular _____ musical instrument.
4 We listened to some good _____ music at the Glastonbury Festival.
5 The Rolling Stones and REM are famous _____ bands.
6 _____ _____ concerts are often very noisy.
7 I think _____ is great dance music.
8 My dad loves Mozart, but I hate _____ music.

3 Complete the sentences with the words below.

concert   weather   festival   music
noise   tent   rock singer ✓

1 My favourite _____ is Bono from U2.
2 My mum always listens to _____ in the car.
3 Diwali is a famous Indian _____ .
4 We love camping and sleeping in a _____ .
5 I can't play my guitar at home because of the loud _____ .
6 The _____ is often terrible at festivals – there is a lot of rain!
7 For my birthday my mum always takes me to a _____ .

Grammar

Past simple: verb *to be*

4 (*) Underline the correct form of the past simple to complete the dialogue.

Jill: [1] *Was/Were* you at the concert last night?
Mark: Yes, I [2] *was/were* there with Katie.
Jill: [3] *Was/Were* Luke with Katie, too?
Mark: No, he [4] *wasn't/weren't*. Luke [5] *was/wasn't* at home with a bad cold.
Jill: [6] *Was/Were* there lots of rock bands?
Mark: Yes, there [7] *was/were*. There [8] *was/were* all kinds of bands.
Jill: [9] *Was/Were* the weather okay?
Mark: No, it [10] *was/wasn't*, it was terrible.

5 (**) Put the words in the correct order to make sentences.

1 music/was/brilliant/the
   The music was brilliant.
2 wasn't/Luke/at the festival
   _____ .
3 Luke/why/at/the festival/wasn't
   _____ ?
4 terrible/the/weather/was
   _____ .
5 a disaster/was/the/concert
   _____ .
6 last night/you/cold/were
   _____ ?

6 (**) Complete the email with the correct form of the verb *to be*.

To: george@gmail34.com
From: lukesmile@dmail.co.uk
Subject: The festival

Hi George!
Thanks for your text I [1] _wasn't_ at the festival with Katie – I [2] _____ in bed with a bad cold but [3] _____ warm and dry! The tickets [4] _____ expensive, too, so I [5] _____ really upset but it [6] _____ a very exciting night. ☹ There [7] _____ some good programmes on TV but all my friends [8] _____ at the festival so I [9] _____ alone ☹.
Luke

7 (✱✱) Look at the poster for Dalesbury 2010. Answer the questions with short answers.

2010 DALESBURY FESTIVAL

2010 Dalesbury Festival Highlights

Friday 27th : New bands competition
Saturday 28th: Tent 1 – Rock bands
Sunday 29th: Tent 2 – Rap and hip-hop bands
Glade Field – Party
Festival Tent – New bands

1 Were there rock bands in tent two?
  No, there weren't.

2 Were there rap bands in tent one?
  _____

3 Were there rock bands in tent one?
  _____

4 Was the party on Saturday night?
  _____

5 Was the new bands competition on Friday night?
  _____

6 Was the party in the festival tent?
  _____

8 (✱✱) Write questions with the past simple tense.

1 Who/with Sarah/yesterday?
  Who was with Sarah yesterday?

2 Where/you/last night?
  _____

3 Why/Sarah/not at concert/last week?
  _____

4 Where/Tom/in January?
  _____

5 Who/at concert/last month?
  _____

6 Why/was/Tom/at home/yesterday?
  _____

Grammar reference

Past simple: verb *to be*

Form

+	I/He/She/It **was** You/We/They **were**	in town yesterday.
–	I/He/She/It **was not (wasn't)** You/We/They **were not (weren't)**	
?	**Was** I/he/she/it **Were** you/we/they	in town yesterday?
Short answers	Yes, he/she/it **was**. No, he/she/it **wasn't**. Yes, you/we/they **were**. No, you/we/they **weren't**.	

Wh- questions	Answers
Where were you yesterday?	I was in town.
Why was she late for school on Monday?	Because the bus was late.
Who was your favourite singer when you were a child?	My favourite singer was Robbie Williams.

Use

We use the past simple to talk about situations in the past.

Time expressions

We can use these time expressions with the past simple:
yesterday, last night/week/month

*I was very tired **yesterday**.*
*They were in Paris **last month**.*
*He wasn't at school **last week**.*
*Where were you **last night**?*

Vocabulary

Festivals

1 **Match the words 1–8 with the words a–h to make phrases.**

1 light	a New Year
2 watch	b special clothes
3 give	c a parade
4 send	d fireworks
5 watch	e special food
6 eat	f emails
7 wear	g presents
8 celebrate	h candles

2 **Complete the crossword.**

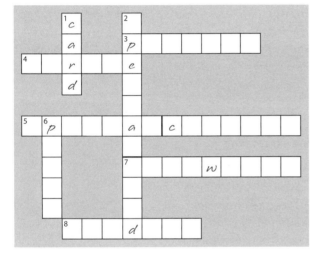

Across

3 You give this to people on their birthday.

4 A public celebration on the streets.

5 You wear these on special occasions.

7 Explosions of colourful lights in the sky.

8 People light these for Diwali.

Down

1 You send this to people on birthdays or at Christmas.

2 You eat this on special occasions.

6 A celebration with food and dancing!

Grammar

Past simple affirmative

3 (*) **Complete the sentences using the correct form of the verbs below.**

> start   wear ✓   clean   decorate
> celebrate   text

1 For Diwali Anisha _wore_ new clothes.

2 I _____ Diwali with Anisha's family this year.

3 We _____ the house with candles.

4 Jamie finally _____ his bedroom!

5 The fireworks display _____ at 9.30.

6 Anisha _____ her sister at midnight.

4 (*) **Complete Jamie's diary with the correct form of the past simple.**

★ 31 DECEMBER

Tonight we went to a fantastic street party in town. I¹ _wore_ (wear) my new jacket – and ² _____ (take) a hat and scarf because it was cold. There were a lot of people and we ³ _____ (dance) all night. At midnight we ⁴ _____ (sing) a traditional song and I ⁵ _____ (send) a text message to my girlfriend Lily to say Happy New Year! We had a brilliant evening, I'm very tired now!

Grammar Plus: Position of time expressions

5 (**) **Put the words in the correct order to make sentences.**

1 you/were/yesterday/where

   Where were you yesterday?

2 went/I/to Scotland/last year

   _____ .

3 in February/New/is/Chinese/Year

   _____ .

4 was/at the party/Peter/last night

   _____ ?

5 in 2007/I/on holiday/to India/went

   _____ .

6 the/started/yesterday/festival

   _____ .

6 (✷✷) Write sentences in the past simple.

1 The party starts at five o'clock.
   The party started at five o'clock.

2 My friend gives me presents at Christmas.
   _____.

3 Oscar goes to Scotland in January.
   _____.

4 They put candles in the garden for Diwali.
   _____.

5 We sing traditional songs on New Year's Eve
   _____.

6 Jamie sends me text messages.
   _____.

7 My dad cooks Christmas dinner.
   _____.

8 Lee's parents tidy and decorate their house for Chinese New Year.
   _____.

7 (✷✷) Complete the text with the correct past simple form of the verbs below.

> have   tidy   start   wear   be ✓
> dance   finish   clean   give   go
> decorate   cook   watch

Notting Hill Festival

This year the Notting Hill festival ¹ *was* really good. Before the parade the organisers ² _____ the streets in beautiful colours and ³ _____ special food to sell to tourists and visitors.

At one o'clock the streets were very busy, there were lots of people. The parade _____ at two o'clock in the afternoon. The children and adults in the parade _____ special clothes they were very colourful and they ⁶ _____ to the traditional music. They _____ free sweets to the children. A lot of tourists _____ the parade and enjoyed the celebrations.

The party ⁹ _____ at around two o'clock in the morning and people ¹⁰ _____ home to sleep. Everybody ¹¹ _____ a great time. The next day volunteers ¹² _____ and ¹³ _____ the streets and Notting Hill was a normal London street again.

Grammar reference

Past simple affirmative (regular and irregular verbs)

Form

Regular verbs

- With most regular verbs we add -*ed* to the infinitive.

listen → listened, paint → painted

- With infinitives ending in -*e*, we only add -*d*.

live → lived, decorate → decorated

- With infinitives ending in a consonant + *y*, -*y* in the past simple affirmative becomes -*ied*.

carry → carried, marry → married

- With infinitives ending in a single vowel + single consonant, we often double the final consonant.

stop → stopped, plan → planned

Irregular verbs

Some verbs are irregular, for example:

give → gave, wear → wore, put → put

go → went, send → sent, hold → held

sing → sang, do → did, see → saw

Use

We use the past simple to talk about actions which started and finished in the past.

*She **married** Tom.*
*I **watched** the film on TV yesterday.*

Time expressions

yesterday, last night/week/Monday/month/year,
three days/weeks/years ago, in March/September, in 2006

*Ann **wore** a nice dress **yesterday**.*
*We **saw** Mark **last Saturday** at the party.*
*The band **gave** their last concert **in August**.*

Position of time expressions

Time expressions can go:

- at the beginning or end of affirmative and negative sentences.

*I went there **three years ago**.*
***Last year**, we spent Christmas in London.*
*They didn't visit Tom **in March 2007**.*

- at the end of questions.

*Did you talk to him **last night**?*
*Where were you **yesterday at five o'clock**?*

Listening

1 (12) Listen to DJ Karen Mace talking to John Connelly. <u>Underline</u> the correct answer.

Traditional Scottish Music

Robbie Burns

1 John Connelly is *Scottish/English*.
2 Robbie Burns died in *1796/1967*.
3 Robbie Burns was a *writer/musician*.
4 On Burn's Night they sing *rock/folk songs*.
5 Burn's Night is on *25th January/20th January*.
6 Burn's Night *is/isn't* the Scottish New Year.

2 (12) Listen again and choose the correct answer.

1 John Connelly is
  a a Scottish writer.   b a Scottish actor.
  c a Scottish singer.

2 Robbie Burns wrote
  a poetry and songs.
  b about Scottish songs.
  c about Scottish food and drink.

3 For dinner on Burn's Night, Scottish people eat
  a meat and vegetables.   b cereals.
  c haggis.

4 After dinner they
  a sing songs and drink whisky.
  b dance and sing songs.
  c read poetry and sing songs.

5 At the end of the evening there is
  a lots of dancing.   b lots of drinking.
  c lots of reading.

6 In Scotland they celebrate New Year
  a in January.   b on Burn's Night.
  c in December.

7 For the street party in Edinburgh
  a tickets are free.
  b you need to buy a ticket.
  c you don't need a ticket.

8 The street party finishes at
  a at one o'clock in the morning.
  b at midnight.   c the next day.

Reading

3 Match the words a–e with their definitions 1–5.

1 raise money (v)
2 success (n)
3 crowd (n)
4 cheer (v)
5 charity (n)

a to collect money to help people
b an organisation that gives money or help to people
c a good result
d a large group of people
e to shout and show support

4 Read the text. Match the headings a–e with the correct paragraph 1–4. There is one extra heading.

a My big day
b Facts
c History
d Olympic champions
e London's sports festival

5 Read the text again and choose the correct answer.

1 How many people finished the first race in 1981?
  a 7,700   b 6,250   c 32,500

2 How many people competed last year?
  a 46,000   b 32,500   c forty-two

3 The London Marathon is
  a forty-two miles.   b forty-one kilometres.
  c twenty-six miles.

4 The roads are closed for
  a twenty-four hours.   b seven hours.
  c twelve hours.

5 Last year
  a half a million people raced.
  b half a million people watched the race on TV.
  c five million people watched the race on TV.

6 Tick (✓) true or cross (✗) false.

1 ☐ The London Marathon started in 1991.
2 ☐ There is a London Marathon every year.
3 ☐ In 1981 all the competitors finished the race.
4 ☐ Most competitors in the London Marathon are English.
5 ☐ The London Marathon is forty-two kilometres long.
6 ☐ The race started at 7.00 in the morning.
7 ☐ Jess wore a funny costume for charity.
8 ☐ Jess finished the race in seven hours.

LONDON MARATHON

Home   Jess Pitcher's Marathon Blog

Jess Pitcher's Marathon Blog

Matt's Training Blog

Jess Pitcher's Marathon Blog

Sarah's Great Triumph

Other links

Contact

Safety

Training

Events

Newsletter

Links

1 _e_

This year was an amazing year for me because of finished the London Marathon!

The London Marathon is more than a race – it's a London sports festival. It is famous all over the world now. Lots of people run in the marathon and many more people watch it on TV.

2 ___

The first London Marathon was on 29th March 1981. A British Olympic runner, Chris Brasher, decided to organise a marathon in London because there was a marathon in New York every year and it was very successful, so he wanted to do the same in London. There were over 7,700 competitors and around 6,250 people finished the race.

3 ___

There is a marathon in London every year and competitors come from all over the world. There are young people like me and old people, too – some are eighty years old! Last year there were more than 46,000 competitors and around 32,500 finished the race.

The distance of the London Marathon is forty-two kilometres or twenty-six miles and that is a very long distance!

There is no traffic, the roads close at 7.00 a.m. and open again at 7.00 p.m.

4 ___

The raced started at 10.00 a.m. and I was very nervous! There were thousands of competitors. Most people wore normal clothes like me but some people wore funny and unusual costumes like Batman or a big banana! Usually people run to raise money for charity. Half a million people watched the race and cheered the competitors, and five million watched on TV! It was amazing! I finished the race at 5.00 p.m. and I had very sore feet, but I still celebrated with some traditional London food – fish and chips – fantastic!

Jess Pitcher, 19

Me training for the London Marathon

Great costumes

festival fever

61

Writing

An informal letter

1 Write your address and the date in the top right corner.

2 Open the letter: *Dear* + name,

3 Start a new paragraph to give and describe new information.

4 Close the letter: *Write and tell me your news, Write soon, Take care, Lots of love*

5 Sign your name.

78 Brooke Street
Queensberry
London
SW4 1AF
26 January 2010

Hi Janya,

How are you? I'm having a great time in London! I'm staying with my friend Ang and her family. They are celebrating Chinese New Year this week so there is lots to do.

Yesterday I had a lot of fun but it was a very busy day. First, we cleaned the house and then we decorated the doors and windows with red paint. Then we cooked some traditional Chinese food with Ang's mum. All the family sat down to eat together and afterwards we talked and played games.

In the evening we went into central London and watched the Chinese dragon parade. I really enjoyed it but I was very tired.

Today there are more parades and dancing. At the moment we're sitting in a restaurant in China Town eating noodles and soup, delicious!

Take care.
Adele

---

1 Read Adele's letter and answer the questions.

1 Where is Adele?

_____.

2 Who is she with?

_____.

3 What are they are celebrating?

_____.

4 What did they eat?

_____.

5 Where did they go in the evening?

_____.

6 How did Adele feel at the end of the evening?

_____.

2 Put the phrases in the correct order.

a ☐ Write soon.

b ☐ How are you?

c ☐ Dear Mary,

d ☐ 28 April 2010

e ☑ 15 Wisbeck Avenue, London, E12 4TR

f ☐ I'm fine. I had a fantastic weekend in Paris. The weather was great and the food was delicious. I stayed with my friend Marie.

g ☐ Lots of love, Alex

3 We organise our ideas in paragraphs. A new paragraph talks about different topics or times. Read Bob's letter and put the paragraphs in the correct order.

Dear James,

a ___ On Saturday morning we visited the modern art gallery with Tom. It was really interesting. Then we had lunch in the town centre.

b ___ We got up early on Sunday and took the train to the coast. It was really beautiful but it was cold. We came home in the afternoon and watched football on TV.

c ___ We went to Trinity College Museum on Saturday afternoon and saw lots of interesting Celtic objects and books. I really enjoyed it.

d _1_ How are you? I'm here in Dublin and having a great time. It's a really interesting city. There are lots of great shops and galleries.

Write and tell me your news.

Bob

4 Read the letter and divide it into three paragraphs.

> How are you? I'm studying English in Edinburgh for the summer. I'm having a great time, it's a brilliant city. The students here are really nice. They are from all over the world. Most of the students are the same age as me so we go out together in the evenings. The school is in the centre of town. There are ten small classrooms and there is a café, a library and a language laboratory.

5 Complete the strategies with the phrases below.

> I hope you're well   I'm having a great time
> Write and tell me your news   Hello ✓

- Start the letter with an informal greeting: *Hi*, ¹ _Hello_ or *Dear* + name
- Ask how the person is: How are you? ² _____
- Describe where you are and what you are doing/did: *Devon is brilliant,* ³ _____
- Organise your letter into paragraphs to add new information.
- Close the letter with a phrase: *Write soon*, *Take care,* ⁴ _____ , *Lots of love.*

6 Read the task and then write your informal letter. Use the strategies in exercise 5 to help you.

> Imagine you went to a music festival last weekend. Write a letter to your friend and tell them about the festival.
> - Write your address and the date.
> - Describe the festival.
> - Write a closing sentence.

Speaking

Buying tickets

7 Match the questions 1–5 with the answers a–e.

1 What time is the next train?
2 What platform is the next train?
3 Can I have a ticket to Bristol, please?
4 How much is it?
5 Is there a student reduction?

a Single or return?
b That's £20, please.
c Yes, there is.
d It's in half and hour, at 12.45.
e Platform 3.

8 Complete the dialogue with the words below.

> start   tickets   What time   How much
> have ✓   student reduction

Sue: Can I ¹ _have_ two ² _____ for *High Street Musical*, please?
Assistant: Certainly.
Sue: ³ _____ are they?
Assistant: Tickets are £7, so that's £14, please.
Sue: Is there a ⁴ _____ ?
Assistant: No, there isn't. Sorry.
Sue: ⁵ _____ does the film ⁶ _____ ?
Assistant: At 8.30.

9 Put the dialogue into the correct order.

a ☐ Is there a student discount?
b ☐ The tickets are £15 each, so that's £30, please.
c ☐ Platform 7 in twenty minutes.
d ☐ Yes, there is. It's £10 for students, so that's £20 for two tickets.
e ☑ *1* Can I have two return tickets to London, please?
f ☐ Here you are. Which platform is the next train?

Vocabulary

Everyday technology

1 Label the names of the objects.

1 _mobile phone_   2 _____

3 _____   4 _____

2 Put the words below in the correct column.

> cooker   alarm clock   electric kettle
> electric toothbrush   hairdryer ✓
> toaster   TV

bedroom	bathroom	kitchen
hairdryer		

3 Which of the items from exercises 1 and 2 do you:

1 watch in the evening? _TV_

2 use to make your breakfast? _____

3 use after you wash your hair? _____

4 use to make a cup of tea? _____

5 use to talk to friends? _____

6 use in the morning to wake you up? _____

Grammar

Past simple negative and questions

4 ** Use the prompts to write sentences.

1 I/not brush/my teeth this morning
   I didn't brush my teeth this morning.

2 The English/not invent/toothbrushes
   _____ .

3 Italians/not wear/make-up 6000 years ago, the Egyptians did
   _____ .

4 People/not watch/TV three hundred years ago
   _____ .

5 This morning/I/not have/ a bowl of cereal for breakfast
   _____ .

6 The Persians/not have/mobile phones
   _____ .

7 The ancient Greeks/not build/the first bicycle
   _____ .

8 2,000 years ago the Germans/not make/ the first battery
   _____ .

5 * Complete the text with the verbs in brackets.

I woke up late this morning and I turned the alarm clock off but I [1] _didn't listen_ (not/listen) to the radio. I brushed my teeth but I [2] _____ (not/eat) cornflakes, I had toast. I was late so I [3] _____ (not/comb) my hair and I [4] _____ (not/say) 'goodbye' to Mum. When I arrived at school I [5] _____ (not/see) my friends and I [6] _____ (not/check) my homework. At 4 p.m. I walked home. I [7] _____ (not/go) by bus because I [8] _____ (not/have) any money.

6 (✱✱) Put the words in the correct order to make questions or negative sentences.

1 read/you/newspaper/did/yesterday/the/?
   Did you read the newspaper yesterday?

2 didn't/eat/Sue/this morning/toast
   _____ .

3 eat/Sue/cereal/did/this morning/?
   _____ ?

4 wear/didn't/Sue/her sunglasses/yesterday
   _____ .

5 the/Egyptians/did/eat rice/6,000 years ago/?
   _____ ?

6 draw/Einstein/didn't/Mickey Mouse
   _____ .

7 Columbus/did/invent/electric light/?
   _____ ?

8 you/text messages/didn't/I/send/any
   _____ .

7 (✱✱) Use the prompts to write questions and answers.

1 Tracy/wear/make-up/last night (✓)
   Did Tracey wear make-up last night?
   Yes, she did.

2 Chinese/invent/paper (✓)
   _____
   _____

3 you/know/the answers/to the quiz (✗)
   _____
   _____

4 Einstein/fail Maths at school (✓)
   _____
   _____

5 Charlie/finish/homework/yesterday (✗)
   _____
   _____

8 (✱✱) Use the prompts to complete the online chat.

ClareKy: Hi Dan, How are you?
DANZ5: Gr8!
ClareKy: You weren't online yesterday. [1] _Did you have_
   (you/have) a busy day?
DANZ5: Yes, [2] _____ (I/do). I studied all day!
ClareKy: Wow! [3] _____ (you/finish) the homework?
DANZ5: No, [4] _____ (I/do). ☹ It was difficult, [5] _____
   (you/understand) it all?
ClareKy: No. I [6] _____ (not/understand) it. I sent you an email.
   [7] _____ (you/check) your emails yesterday?
DANZ5: Yes, [8] _____ (I/do). I sent you a text message,
   [9] _____ (you/read) it?
ClareKy: No, [10] _____ (I/do). Sorry, I lost my phone last week ☹.

Grammar reference

Past simple negative and questions

Form

	I/You/He/She/It/We/They **cooked**	dinner yesterday.
+		
−	I/You/He/She/It/We/They **didn't cook**	
?	**Did** I/you/he/she/it we/they **cook**	dinner yesterday?

Short answers	Yes, I/you/he/she/it/we/they **did**. No, I/you/he/she/it/we/they **didn't**.

Did you *go* the party last night?
Yes, I *did*.
Did they *make* a cake yesterday?
No, they *didn't*. They *didn't have* time.
Did Sam *talk* to Lisa yesterday?
No, he *didn't*. He *didn't go* to school.

Vocabulary

Modern science

1 **Rearrange the words to complete the sentences.**

1 Alexander Fleming _discovered_ (vdscioeedr) antibiotics.

2 Les Paul _____ (evdlodpee) the electric guitar.

3 Dr Martin Cooper _____ (veintedn) the mobile phone.

4 Jean Nouvel _____ (geidnsde) the Louvre museum in Paris.

5 The Ancient Egyptians _____ (tubil) the pyramids.

2 **Complete the text about Professor Fess with the correct form of the words below.**

> develop   design   build   discover
> invent ✓

This is Professor Fess – he thinks he's a genius.

He always has new ideas and he loves

¹ _inventing_ things.

Last year he ² _____ his own eco car and his

friend Mikey the mechanic ³ _____ it.

Professor Fess says he is also ⁴ _____ a new

green energy source in the Amazon rainforests.

Now he wants to ⁵ _____ a way for everybody

to use this new energy.

Grammar

Past simple + question words

3 (✳) **Match the question words 1–7 with the questions a–g.**

1 Where   a discovered electricity?

2 How many   b did Einstein live? In Germany.

3 What   c did Alexander Bell invent the telephone?

4 Who   d did the Ancient Egyptians build?

5 Why   e did people communicate before the invention of the Internet?

6 When   f is Leonardo da Vinci famous?

7 How   g paintings did Leonardo da Vinci complete?

4 (✳) **Complete the dialogue with the questions below.**

> What did you do there?
> Who did you go with?
> Where did you have lunch?
> Where did you go? ✓
> How did you get there?

Ana: I had a great time on holiday last year.

John: ¹ _Where did you go?_

Ana: I went to Galway on the west coast of Ireland.

John: ² _____

Ana: I travelled by Ferry from Liverpool to Dublin and then I took a coach to Galway.

John: ³ _____

Ana: I went with my cousin Julia. It was her first time in Ireland, too.

John: ⁴ _____

Ana: One day we went horse riding and another day we tried windsurfing, and on the last day we went to the Galway races. It was brilliant.

John: ⁵ _____
We usually ate in the pubs and had fresh fish and Irish bread.

5 (✱✱) Write questions for the answers. The words in bold help you.

1 _What did you buy?_
   I bought a **book**.

2 _____ ?
   I went to the museum **yesterday**.

3 _____ ?
   I saw **Tim** in the café.

4 _____ ?
   I went to school **by bus**.

5 _____ ?
   I met Jane **in the café**.

6 _____ ?
   I listened to the radio **because** the TV didn't work.

7 _____ ?
   I spent **£10**.

8 _____ ?
   I did **two** English exercises.

Grammar Plus: *which* and *what*

6 (✱) Complete the questions with *what* or *which*.

1 _____ food do you like?

2 _____ flavour did you prefer, apple or orange?

3 _____ train goes to Leeds?

4 _____ music do you listen to?

5 _____ book did you choose?

6 _____ books do you like to read?

7 (✱✱) Write questions for the answers.

1 Who _designed the webpage_ ?
   James designed the webpage.

2 Who _____ ?
   The French developed Gothic architecture.

3 Who _____ ?
   I visited my best friend.

4 Who _____ ?
   The teacher gave Tom extra homework.

5 Who _____ ?
   Gabriel helped Tom.

6 Who _____ ?
   I saw the accident.

Grammar reference

Past simple + question words

Form

We put question words at the beginning of a *wh*-question:

Where did you study? → At Cambridge University.
What did they have for lunch? → Fish and chips.
Which bus do you take to school: 3b or 5a? → 3b.
What time did she go to bed? → At 11 p.m.
When did the film start? → At 5 p.m.
How did he go to work? → By taxi.
Why did you come to school so late? → Because my mother didn't wake me up.
How much did she pay for her new dress? → £20.
Who did you meet at the cinema? → Mark and Jane.

We use *what* in very general questions and *which* in questions with a limited choice of answers:

What books do you like?
(in general, there are many kinds of books to choose from)
Which is your pen: the red one or the blue one?
(a limited choice, only two pens to choose from)

Notice!

What films do you like?
Which film did you like more: Shrek 3 or Madagascar?

Subject and object questions

Questions with *who* and *what* can be subject or object questions. Subject questions have the form of an affirmative sentence (we don't use *did*).

	subject	**object**
	↓	↓

Larry Page and Sergey Brin created   *Google.*

Subject question:
Who created Google? → Larry Page and Sergey Brin.

Object question:
What did Larry Page and Sergey Brin **create**? → Google.

	subject	**object**
	↓	↓

Robert danced   with *Elizabeth* all the time.

Subject question:
Who danced with Elizabeth all the time? → Robert.

Object question:
Who did Robert **dance** with all the time? → Elizabeth.

Vocabulary

Inventions

1 Read the sentences and match them with the words below. There are two items you do not need.

> the Internet   the mobile phone ✓
> the hairdryer   the aeroplane   the radio
> the MP3 player

1

> *I can't live without it. I use it every day to speak to friends and family. It is so easy to communicate now.*

the mobile phone

2

> *It is a fantastic form of transport – people can travel easily all over the world whenever they want.*

_____

3

> *I can download music and listen to all my favourite songs. It's very light and very easy to use.*

_____

4

> *I use it to do my homework, my mum uses it to do online shopping and my sister uses it to chat with friends. It's really useful.*

_____

2 Write in the missing letters to complete the text.

The way we use technology now

So many objects now have more than one function and technology is changing fast. Most people have a ¹m _obile phone_ and they use it to talk to their friends. They also use it to listen to music, too so they don't need an ²M _ _ p _ _ _ _ r. There are ³c _ _ _ u t _ _ _ now in every home, and people use them to surf the ⁴In _ _ _ _ _ _ but they can also use them to watch ⁵T _ . and listen to the ⁶r _ _ _ o. It's amazing. Technology and the way we use it is changing very fast. The only bad thing about this new technology is that it uses a lot of ⁷e _ _ c _ _ _ _ _ _ y and this is expensive for us!

technology

Reading

3 Read the text quickly. Which picture is each paragraph about?

4 Read the text and match the headings 1–3 with the paragraphs a–c.
1 Toilet humour
2 I can see properly!
3 Convenience food

inventions that really changed the way we live.

When we talk about inventions many people think of modern technology but the important inventions that changed our lives are a bit more basic.

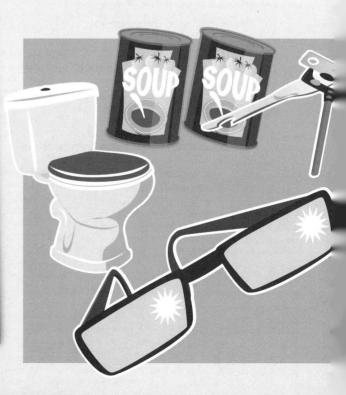

5 Read the text again and tick (✓) true or cross (✗) false.

1 ☐ In 1262 Roger Bacon discovered that glass can help you see.

2 ☐ Roger Bacon invented the first pair of glasses.

3 ☐ The first tin opener was difficult to use.

4 ☐ William Lyman invented the first tin opener in 1870.

5 ☐ Toilets were popular in England during the time of Queen Elizabeth I.

6 ☐ Alexander Cummings developed a new toilet design.

Can you imagine life without glasses? Many people have problems with their eyes and they need glasses. In 1262 Roger Bacon discovered that glass can help you see and an Italian inventor, Alessandro di Spina, made the first pair of glasses in 1282. These glasses were very different from the glasses we wear today but they were a really useful invention.

How did people open soup before the invention of the tin opener?! This small invention changed the way we eat and what we buy. In the 1860's Ezra Warner created the first tin opener. This was an amazing invention but only shopkeepers had them as they were too big to have at home and difficult to use. Shopkeepers opened the tins for the customers before they left the shop. Finally, in 1870 William Lyman invented the modern tin opener so everybody could open tins at home.

What about the modern toilet, can you imagine life before the invention of the toilet? In the past, people went outside to use the toilet so modern toilets are much more convenient. Sir John Harington invented the first toilet for Queen Elizabeth I in 1596 but people thought it was a joke and it wasn't popular. Two hundred years later Alexander Cummings developed a new design and the toilet became popular. Now everybody has a toilet.

Listening

6 (13) Listen to Nadia presenting her school project and complete the notes about Samuel Houghton

Name: Samuel Houghton
Age:
Home town: Buxton
Invention: Broom
Use of invention:
Where Nadia got her information:

7 (13) Listen again and choose the correct answer.

1 Nadia chose Samuel Houghton because
   a he is a very young inventor.
   b she knows him.
   c he invented a kind of brush.

2 Samuel Houghton invented the broom
   a to help his dad.
   b to make money.
   c to become famous.

3 Samuel Houghton invented the broom when he was
   a three years old.
   b five years old.
   c six years old.

4 Samuel wants to produce
   a new technology.
   b beautiful things.
   c useful things.

5 Samuel Houghton's father
   a started a programme in schools about inventions.
   b started a programme in schools about business.
   c started a programme in schools about money.

6 Nadia read about Samuel Houghton
   a on the Internet.
   b in a magazine.
   c in a newspaper.

Reading

Multiple choice

The questions follow the order of the information in the text. Look for the same information in different words.

1 Read the beginning of Tom's story and questions 1–2. Use the underlined words in the story to choose the best option a, b or c.

How I met my girlfriend

I first met my girlfriend Mary on the Internet, on a website for music fans. Not many people listen to the same kind of music as I do, especially not many girls ... A lot of people just don't know the bands I like. And I saw this girl's profile on the website, and she liked them all! I wrote her a message and she replied. And guess what? We discovered that we went to the same school!

The next day I met her at school and she was really pretty. She looked beautiful in her old jeans and black jumper. I thought, 'This is fantastic: she's pretty and she likes my favourite music and she likes me!'

1 Why did Tom write to Mary?
  a He liked her photo on the website.
  b They had the same interests.
  c They went to the same school.

2 What did Tom discover when he met Mary?
  a She liked his favourite music.
  b She was good-looking.
  c She wore beautiful clothes.

2 Match the *wrong* answers in exercise 1 to the reasons why they are wrong.
  a ☐ He discovered that before.
  b ☐ He didn't know that when he wrote to her.
  c ☐ She didn't; she wore old jeans.
  d ☐ He doesn't say anything about a photo.

3 Read the end of Tom's story and choose the best option a, b or c.

We talked every day at school. We didn't walk home together because she lives in a different part of the town. Then one Saturday we went to a gig. It was a new band. The tickets were expensive, the weather was terrible and the music wasn't very good .... But we were happy just because we were together.

Now we go everywhere together: to concerts, to the cinema, to music festivals, to film festivals. It's great to have a girlfriend who is your best friend.

1 Where did Tom and Mary meet every day?
  a They met at school.
  b They walked home together.
  c They went to gigs.

2 Why did Tom like the concert?
  a Because the music was great.
  b Because the tickets were cheap.
  c Because he was with Mary.

Listening

True/False

If one piece of information in a statement is false, the statement is false.

4 (14) Listen to the first part of Tricia and Dave's conversation. Tick (✓) true or cross (✗) false. Listen again and correct the false information.
  1 ☐ Dave is waiting for Tricia at the cinema.
  2 ☐ Dave is twenty minutes late.
  3 ☐ Tricia and Dave are in two different places.

5 (15) Listen twice to the rest of the conversation. Tick (✓) true or cross (✗) false.
  1 ☐ Tricia orders a chicken salad.
  2 ☐ Dave wants to drink water and coffee.
  3 ☐ A piece of carrot cake is £2.50.
  4 ☐ Tricia doesn't order cake.

Use of English

Jumbled sentences

Exam TIP

When you are putting jumbled sentences in order, remember:
- Check if the sentence is a *statement* or a *question*. The word order is different.
- Notice collocations.

6 Put the words in the correct order to make phrases.

1 favourite/singer/my

my favourite singer

2 cake/a/of/piece

_____

3 music/to/listen

_____

4 to/easy/use

_____

5 new/meet/people

_____

6 a/wear/jacket

_____

7 the/at/party

_____

7 Put the words in the correct order to make sentences. The first word is there for you.

1 favourite/who/actor/your/is

Who *is your favourite actor* ?

2 listening/to/am/music/I

I _____ .

3 I/have/a piece/carrot cake/of/can

Can _____ ?

4 phone/use/this/is/to/mobile/easy

This _____ .

5 people/you/meeting/do/new/like

Do _____ ?

6 is/jacket/he/a/wearing/not

He _____ .

7 party/do/at/did/the/what/they

What _____ ?

Speaking

Photo description

8 Look at the photo and answer the questions.

1 Who is in the photo?

Three *teenagers* .

2 Where are they?

In a _____ .

3 What are they doing?

They are _____ at something on a laptop.

9 Complete the description with the verbs below in the present continuous tense.

> chat   look ✓   read   sit   stand
> study   watch

In the photo I can see three boys or young men in a library. I know this is a library because there are a lot of books in the background. In the centre of the photo there is a laptop on a table and the boys [1] *are looking* at it. Two of them [2] _____ at the table and one [3] _____ . There are some books on the table, so maybe the boys [4] _____ … but I don't think so. I think they can see something funny on the screen – perhaps they're looking at a photo or [5] _____ a film or [6] _____ a funny blog, or [7] _____ with a friend.

Exam TIP

Say *who* is in the photo, *where they are* and *what they are doing*. Use the present continuous tense to say what people are doing.

exam trainer 2

self-assessment test 4

Vocabulary & Grammar

1 Rearrange the letters to make the names of seven types of music.

1 z a j z   _jazz_
2 c r k o   _____
3 k o f l   _____
4 k u n p   _____
5 i p h-h p o   _____
6 i o s c d   _____
7 c a l l a i s s c   _____

/6

2 Match the words 1–6 from column A with the correct nouns a–f from column B.

A   B
1 music   a phone
2 electric   b dancing
3 mobile   c clock
4 heavy   d toothbrush
5 alarm   e metal
6 traditional   f festival

/5

3 Complete the sentences with the words below.

cards ✓   fireworks   party   candles
parade   way   hairdryer

1 Every year I get a lot of _cards_ and presents for my birthday.
2 The invention of the computer changed the _____ we live.
3 On New Year's Eve we usually go to the city centre and watch amazing _____ .
4 Do you usually go to a _____ on New Year's Eve or do you stay at home?
5 Sara's eight today so there are eight _____ on her birthday cake.
6 There was a big _____ in the streets yesterday. More than 250 people walked through the town centre.
7 I wash my hair every day but I never use a _____ .

/6

4 Complete the sentences with the past simple form of the verbs in brackets.

1 I _texted_ (text) you an hour ago.
2 Last year we _____ (go) on holiday to Spain.
3 The concert yesterday _____ (be) brilliant.
4 I _____ (not finish) my essay last night.
5 _____ (you/wear) this dress to the party?
6 Robert _____ (make) a cake on Sunday!
7 They _____ (not be) here yesterday.
8 I _____ (give) you my pen two days ago.
9 _____ (they/talk) about me at the party?

/8

5 Write past simple questions for the answers in bold.

1 _What time did the film start?_
The film started **at 7 p.m.**
2 _____ ?
I saw them **at the party**.
3 _____ ?
My grandparents sold their house **in February**.
4 _____ ?
Larry Page and Sergey Brin created Google.
5 _____ ?
I read **three books** last month.
6 _____ ?
I talked **to my History teacher** after the lesson.

/5

Listening

6 (16) Listen to three friends talking about their school science project. Answer the questions with their names: Pete (P), Debbie (D) or Michael (M)
Who:

1 doesn't want to write about a modern invention? ____
2 finished writing his/her project? ____
3 didn't know who invented Google? ____
4 knows somebody who doesn't use a mobile phone? ____
5 thinks modern inventions changed the way we live? ____

/5

Reading

7 Read the newspaper article and choose the correct answers a, b or c.

Cheese Rolling Festival

The Cooper's Hill Cheese Rolling Festival happens every year in May near the cities of Cheltenham and Gloucester in England. Somebody rolls a large Double Gloucester cheese from the top of the hill and a lot of people race down the hill after it. Cheese Rolling on Cooper's Hill has a very long tradition. It started in the early 1800s.

In the past, there were four races at the Cheese Rolling Festival. But in 2006 there was one extra race because so many people came to Gloucester and wanted to take part in the event. So now there's an extra race every year. The 3rd race is always Ladies' Race (only for women).

The winner of the race gets the cheese, the second prize is £10 and the third £5. But people don't come to win. Some enter the competition but many more come to watch. Hundreds of people love it and everybody has a lot of fun. Competitors and journalists travel from all over the world to be at the festival, including Brazil, the USA, Germany and Australia. In 2008 two actors came to Cooper's Hill and finished their races ... last!

In Cheese Rolling 2008, the first three ladies were: Flo Early, Carly Johnston and Blythe Jopling. The winner – Flo Early – was a student from Painswick.

But Cheese Rolling is not fun for everybody. Some people think it's very dangerous. There are lots of accidents during the festival and Gloucester Royal Hospital has a lot of work. Mark Cooper from Birmingham was 4th in 2008 but after the race he had two operations on his knee. Coming out of hospital he said: 'I'm OK now. I don't feel pain in my knee anymore and my dream now is to win that cheese next year.'

1 In the article, Gloucester is the name of
   a a city and a hill.
   b a city and a type of cheese.
   c a type of cheese and a hill.

2 In 2006 there were ___ cheese rolling races.
   a three   b four   c five

3 Every year ___ come to the festival.
   a hundreds of people
   b people from many countries
   c many famous people

4 Carly Johnston won ___ in Cheese Rolling 2008.
   a £10   b the cheese   c £5

5 Mark Cooper
   a didn't finish the race in 2008.
   b wants to come to the Festival again.
   c felt OK after the race.

/5

Communication

8 Complete the dialogue with one word in each gap.

Liz: Can I have three [1] _tickets_ to London Victoria, please?

Man: Single or [2] _____ ?

Liz: Single, please. Is there a student [3] _____ ?

Man: Yes, there is. The student tickets are £2.50 [4] _____ . So that's £7.50, please.

Liz: Here you are. What platform is the next [5] _____ ?

Man: Platform eleven, in ten minutes.

Liz: Thanks.

/4

9 Use the words in brackets to write questions about your friend's weekend.

1 (go) _Where did you go at the weekend_ ?
   I went to Paris.

2 (how) _____ ?
   I went by train.

3 (who) _____ ?
   With my parents.

4 (do) _____ ?
   We visited the Louvre Museum.

5 (enjoy) _____ ?
   Oh, yes. Very much.

/4

10 Underline the correct words to complete the sentences.

A: What do you [1] think/opinion is the most modern invention?

B: I [2] 'm not/don't sure. Perhaps the computer or the TV.

A: The computer or the TV? I don't [3] think/agree. For me it's electricity.

B: Well, perhaps you're right.

/2

Marks

Vocabulary & Grammar	/30 marks
Listening	/5 marks
Reading	/5 marks
Communication	/10 marks
Total:	/50 marks

go green!

Vocabulary

Green lifestyle

1 Write the words below next to the correct verb.

> bottles ✓   taps   paper   computer
> batteries   lights   packaging   the TV

bottles
|
|
——— recycle ———
|
|
|
——— turn on/off ———
|

2 Complete the poster with the words below.

> environment   the lights   turn off
> plastic   glass   recycling   greener ✓
> batteries

NOTICE TO ALL STUDENTS!

We want King Edwards' school to be [1] *greener* .
We want all students to follow these simple rules:

★ Put all [2] _____ bottles and bags in the green bins.
★ Don't bring [3] _____ bottles to school –
   they can be dangerous.
★ Collect any waste paper and put it in the
   [4] _____ bins.
★ Turn off [5] _____ when you leave the classrooms.
★ Don't throw your used [6] _____ away
   with normal rubbish.
★ Always [7] _____ the taps in the bathrooms.

Let's make our school a greener place and help protect
the [8] _____ .

Grammar

Comparative adjectives

3 ★ Complete the table with the comparative form of the adjectives.

1	green	*greener*
2	good	
3	old	
4	bad	
5	convenient	
6	easy	
7	big	
8	expensive	
9	small	
10	healthy	

4 ★ Complete the sentences with the correct comparative form of the adjectives in brackets.

1 A car is _faster_ than a bus but a bus is
   cheaper . (fast/cheap)
2 A laptop is _____ than a traditional
   computer but it's also _____ .
   (expensive/light)
3 Salad is _____ than pizza but pizza is
   _____ . (healthy/nice)
4 Air travel is _____ than the train but the
   train is _____ . (convenient/green)
5 Badminton is _____ then tennis but
   tennis is _____ . (easy/good)
6 English is _____ than Italian but Chinese
   is _____ . (difficult/bad)
7 My village is _____ than the city but the
   city is _____ . (beautiful/exciting)
8 Marie is _____ than me but
   I'm _____ . (tall/healthy)

5 (******) Complete the sentences with the correct form of the comparative adjectives below.

> tall   expensive   old   big   fast ✓
> cheap

1 A Ferrari can travel at 200 kilometres per hour. A horse can travel at 30 kilometres per hour.
   A Ferrari is _faster_ than a horse.

2 My dad is forty-two, my mum is forty-nine.
   My mum is _____ than my dad.

3 A CD player costs £30. An MP3 player costs £100.
   A CD player is _____ than an MP3 player.

4 A train ticket costs £50. A coach ticket costs £10.
   A train ticket is _____ than a coach ticket.

5 The Empire State Building is 1,250 feet. The Eiffel Tower is 990 feet.
   The Empire State Building is _____ than the Eiffel Tower.

6 A football field is a hundred metres long. A tennis court is twenty-four metres long.
   A football field is _____ than a tennis pitch.

Grammar Plus: Spelling of regular comparative adjectives

6 (******) Read Emily's email. Complete the gaps with the correct comparative form of the adjectives below.

> cheap   fast   green ✓   safe   healthy
> happy   easy

To: fred@gemail34.co.uk
From: jen@gemail32.co.uk
Subject: School eco rules

Hi Fred,
Do you know the school's new eco rules? We want our school to be ¹ _greener_ than other schools. The eco rules say that it is ² _____ not to bring glass bottles into school because they are dangerous. So we bring plastic bottles and recycle them. We also walk to school now – this is ³ _____ because the bus costs £1.50. It's also better for the environment and ⁴ _____ for students, too but some students say that the bus is ⁵ _____ than walking and they don't want to be late for school. There are special coloured bins for different types of recycling – this makes it ⁶ _____ to find where to put your rubbish. Everyone at school is ⁷ _____ because we are doing something to help the environment!
Bye for now,
Jen

Grammar reference

Comparative adjectives

Form

Adjectives	Comparatives
one syllable	add -*er*
old	old**er**
clean	clean**er**
one syllable ending in -*e*	add -*r*
large	larg**er**
nice	nic**er**
one syllable ending in single vowel + single consonant	double the final consonant and add -*er*
slim	slim**mer**
hot	hot**ter**
one or two syllable ending in -*y*	change -*y* into -*ier*
dry	dr**ier**
happy	happ**ier**
two or more syllables	add *more* before the adjective
interesting	**more** interesting
dangerous	**more** dangerous
irregular	
good	better
bad	worse

Use

We use comparative adjectives to compare two (or more) things or people. When you make comparisons using the comparative form, add *than* after the adjective.

*Jessica is **prettier than** me.*
*This book is **more interesting than** that one.*
*Your house **is bigger than** mine.*
*Who **is more intelligent**: Mark or Tim?*
*Tom and James **are taller than** me.*

Vocabulary

Go green

1 Complete the sentences with the words below.

> pollution   hurricane   solar power ✓
> droughts   save   rainforest   floods
> destroy

1 Light from the sun produces _solar power_ .
2 A _____ is a large area of tropical woodland.
3 Some African countries don't have a lot of rain and this can cause _____ .
4 If it rains a lot there are a lot of _____ .
5 Turn off the lights to _____ energy.
6 Cars and planes produce a lot of air _____ .
7 People _____ the rainforests for wood.
8 A _____ is a very big wind and rain storm.

Weather

2 Look at the weather map. Complete the weather forecast with the words below.

> cloudy ✓   rainy   windy   snowy
> foggy   sunny

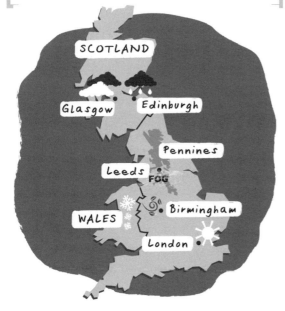

Weather Forecast

Monday 21 April

Today in Scotland it will be cool. In Glasgow it will be ¹c _loudy_ and in Edinburgh it will be ²r_____ . Please take your umbrella today! In Leeds it will be ³f_____ . In Birmingham it will be very ⁴w_____ and in Wales the temperature will be very cold and it will be ⁵s_____ all day. It will be nice in London today – it will be ⁶s_____ all day.

Grammar

will for predictions

3 (✱) Look at the weather map in exercise 2. Answer the questions using short answers.

1 Will it be rainy in London?
   No, it won't.
2 Will it be snowy in Wales?
   _____ .
3 Will it be warm in Scotland?
   _____ .
4 Will it be foggy in Leeds?
   _____ .
5 Will it be windy in Birmingham?
   _____ .
6 Will it be cloudy in Glasgow?
   _____ .

4 (✱✱) Put the words in the correct order to make questions.

1 global warming/will/be worse/in the future
   Will global warming be worse?
2 become/will/pollution/a bigger problem
   _____ ?
3 help to/scientists/will/save the world
   _____ ?
4 will/what/be/weather/like/the
   _____ ?
5 rainforests/we/all/destroy/the/will
   _____ ?
6 droughts/we/will/have/in the future
   _____ ?

5 (✱) Complete the predictions using the correct form of *will* and the verbs in brackets.

1 Most people think things _will be_ (be) worse in the future.
2 Governments _____ (not/be able to) stop global warming.
3 In Africa droughts _____ (become) more common.
4 I don't believe we _____ (destroy) all the rainforests.
5 In the future many countries _____ (use) wind power.
6 Walking to school _____ (not/stop) pollution.
7 I think scientists _____ (develop) more powerful solar energy.

6 (✱✱) Put the questions in the correct place to complete the dialogue.

a Why do you think there will be droughts in Africa?

b Do you think there will be floods?

c What do you think the weather will be like in the future? ✓

d Do you think it will be hotter?

e Do you think there will be more natural disasters?

f What will the weather be like in the UK?

g Where do you think there will be droughts?

h Do you think scientists can stop global warming?

Chris: ¹ _What do you think the weather will be like in_
the future?

Anne: I'm not sure.

Chris: ² _____

Anne: Yes, I think the weather will be very hot.

Chris: Really? ³ _____

Anne: Yes, I do. I think there will be more droughts and hurricanes in the future.

Chris: ⁴ _____

Anne: I think there will be droughts in Africa.

Chris: ⁵ _____

Anne: Africa is already a hot country, global warming will make it hotter and cause droughts.

Chris: ⁶ _____

Anne: No, I think that everybody needs to help to stop global warming, not just scientists.

Chris: ⁷ _____

Anne: I'm not sure but I suppose there will be a lot more rain and it is very rainy now!

Chris: ⁸ _____

Anne: Yes, there definitely will be, more rain will mean more floods.

7 (✱✱) Complete the sentences with *will* or *won't* and the verbs below.

[meet   not like   feel   have ✓   hear]

This week the stars are looking very good for Leo. You ¹ _will have_ a successful day and you ² _____ lots of interesting people. Be careful – you ³ _____ everything you hear today, you ⁴ _____ some bad news and you ⁵ _____ worried.

[be (x2)   need   change   not be]

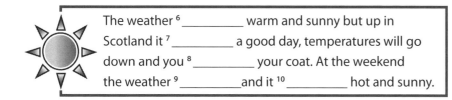

The weather ⁶ _____ warm and sunny but up in Scotland it ⁷ _____ a good day, temperatures will go down and you ⁸ _____ your coat. At the weekend the weather ⁹ _____ and it ¹⁰ _____ hot and sunny.

Grammar reference

will for predictions

Form

+	I/You/He/She/It/We/They **will**	move to Australia.
–	I/You/He/She/It/We/They **will not** (**won't**)	
?	**Will** I/you/he/she/it/we/they	move to Australia?

Short answers	Yes, I/you/he/she/it/we/they **will**.
	No, I/you/he/she/it/we/they **won't**.

Wh- questions	Answers
Where will you go next summer?	I think I'll go to go Portugal.
How much will food cost in five years?	I'm not sure but I think food will cost more in the future.
How will people communicate in the future?	I think people will communicate more online in the future.

Use

We use *will/won't* to say what we think will happen in the future.

*In the future, I think there **will be** more floods and hurricanes.*
*We **won't finish** this project next week.*
*How **will** the weather **change** in the next twenty years?*

Time expressions

in (the next) two/five/ten years,
next week/month/year,
by next Tuesday/2050, in the future

Vocabulary

Go green

1 Match the words in column A with the words in column B to make environment words.

A	B
1 cycle	a pollution
2 global	b spaces
3 green	c zones
4 litter	d lane
5 air	e bin
6 traffic free	f warming

2 Put the environment vocabulary into the correct category.

> cycle lanes ✓   litter bins   traffic
> quieter buses   air pollution
> green spaces   traffic free zones

good for the environment	bad for the environment
cycle lanes	

3 Complete the sentences with the correct words from exercise 2.

1 Riding your bike in town can be dangerous because there aren't any _cycle lanes_ .

2 I think _____ are a great idea, our city is so noisy.

3 Traffic causes _____ and that makes our city an unhealthy place.

4 We need more _____ for children to play and people to walk and sit outside.

5 Rubbish is a problem in our school, we need more _____ .

6 You can't take your car into _____ .

Reading

4 Look at the photos. What do you think the article will be about? Read the article and choose a title.

a Motorists support new speed limits
b Resident stops traffic
c Comedy show in road

5 Read the first part of the article and underline the correct answer.

1 Traffic in Oxford is not *better/worse* than other UK towns.

2 It is more *difficult/easier* for cyclists to use the road.

3 Ted wants people to drive *slower/faster*.

4 Ted thinks motorists will be *surprised/angry* about his protest.

5 Ted put his *furniture/bicycle* in the road.

6 Ted hopes the government will introduce more *cycle lanes/more bicycles* on the roads.

PROBLEMS IN OXFORD

Part 1

Oxford is a beautiful city but the traffic is very bad and a lot of people think the roads are dangerous and that it is more difficult for cyclists to use the roads in Oxford than in other UK cities. So Ted Dewan, a local resident in Oxford, decided to start a personal protest to make the streets of Oxford safer and cleaner.

Ted wants people to drive slower and he wants to stop air and noise pollution, too. He thinks of funny and creative ways to stop or slow traffic. He thinks motorists will be surprised when they see these strange things and they will drive with more care.

One day he moved his living room furniture into the road and watched TV in the street. Another day he put a double bed in the road to slow the traffic. He also put a giant rabbit in the road!

Ted thinks the government will see his protest and introduce more cycle lanes and traffic free zones in Oxford.

Part 2
What do the residents think?

> *Traffic is a problem in this town but it isn't because people drive fast. It's because the roads are busy and people need their cars to get to work. I think drivers will be very angry about these silly protests.*
>
> **Mary, 34**

> *Cars are noisy, they create pollution and they make our town dirtier. Ted's protest will show people that they don't need to use their cars every day and speed limits will stop accidents on our roads.*
>
> **John, 40**

6 Read the second part of the article. Who thinks these things? Write John (J), Ted (T) or Mary (M).

1 Cars create a lot of pollution. ____
2 The roads are busy in Oxford. ____
3 People don't need to use their cars every day. ____
4 Air pollution is a problem in Oxford. ____
5 Drivers will not be happy about the protest. ____
6 People need their cars to get to work. ____
7 Oxford needs more cycle lanes. ____
8 Speed limits will stop accidents. ____

Listening

7 How green is your lifestyle? Read the list below and tick the things you do.

1 ☐ Recycle paper
2 ☐ Recycle plastic
3 ☐ Ride a bike or walk
4 ☐ Turn off lights
5 ☐ Recycle old batteries
6 ☐ Try to use less water

8 (17) Listen and complete the gaps with David (D), Sarah (S) or Emma (E).

1 ____ thinks a lot of people worry but don't do anything about the environment.
2 ____ thinks the weather will become worse in the future.
3 ____ doesn't recycle paper at home.
4 ____ thinks bikes are faster than cars.
5 ____ tries to save water.
6 ____ worries about global warming.

9 (17) Listen again and complete the table with the green things David, Sarah and Emma do and don't do.

How green is your lifestyle?		
	Positive	**Negative**
Sarah	cycles, does not use cars or buses	
David		goes to school by car
Emma		
School	special recycling bins	

Writing

A notice

1 Give your notice a title: *Lost, Found*

2 Say what the object is: *Mobile phone, Keys*

3 Describe the object: *a silver watch, a black and white cat*

4 Say where you lost or found the object: *I lost them at the gym, I left it in the café*

5 Leave your name and contact details: *Call me on 788 233446, Send me an email at Asif@stmail.com*

a

LOST

My new trainers.

They are red and black. They are new and they were a birthday present from my mum.
I lost them at the Abbey Road Gym yesterday afternoon.

Please text me on 788 2334467

Thanks

Dave

b

Found

A silver girl's watch.

I found it in the school canteen on Friday afternoon.

Is it yours?

Send me an email at Asif@stmail.com

Asif

c

Lost!

My pet cat

She is small and white and has got black ears.

I lost her on Tuesday afternoon after school.

I think she ran into Roundhay Park.

Do you know where she is?

765 9987960.

Reward of £30!

Linda

1 Read the notices a–c. Who:

1 lost some trainers? _____

2 didn't lose anything? _____

3 lost a present? _____

4 lost an animal? _____

5 offers a reward? _____

6 was in the school canteen on Friday? _____

2 Complete the notices opposite with the words below.

> Reward   call   blue   send me
> lost   Monday   5.30   yellow ✓
> phone numbers   important

LOST

My address book. It's ¹ *yellow* and white.
It's got all my friends' ² _____ in it.
It's really ³ _____ to me!
I think I ⁴ _____ it at the Cerel Road Youth
Centre on Sunday at ⁵ _____ .
Please ⁶ _____ me on 0112 7654321.
⁷ _____ of £15.
Janet

FOUND

A ⁸ _____ jacket. I found it in the Clarey Café
on Vernon Road on ⁹ _____ .
You can ¹⁰ _____ an email at
kilgy@voogle.com
Kate

3 In short notices it is important to include key information. Look at the notices a–d and say which text does not include:

1 Contact details _c_
2 Where they lost the object ___
3 When they lost the object ___
4 A description of the object ___
5 The name of the object ___

(a) **Lost**
My bag. It was a present from my dad. I lost it at the Envys concert on Saturday. Please text me on 347 43009988. Harry

(b) **A coat**
It's red and black. I left it in the art gallery café on Wednesday afternoon. Please call me on 750 639108.

(c) **Found**
A wallet. It's grey and white with a pink dog on it. I found it in Denison Park. Is it yours? Call me. Mandy

(d) **Lost**
It's small and black. It was a birthday present and I love it. Please call me on 01267 83569827. Mark

4 Complete the strategies box with the phrases below.

[title ✓ contact when Describe
what]

A notice

- Give your notice a short ¹ _title_ : Lost, Found
- Say ² _____ you lost or found: an object, mobile phone
- ³ _____ the object: old, new, red, small
- Say where and ⁴ _____ you lost/found the object.
- Include ⁵ _____ details and your name.

5 Read the task and then write your notice. Use the strategies in exercise 4 to help you.

Choose an object and write a 'Lost' notice.
- Say what you lost.
- Describe the object.
- Say where you lost it.

Speaking

At the shops

6 Complete the dialogue.

Lucy: Hello, excuse me?
Assistant: Yes, can I ¹ _help_ you?
Lucy: I'm ² _____ for a new pair of trainers.
Assistant: OK, what ³ _____ are you?
Lucy: I think I'm a thirty-eight.
Assistant: ⁴ _____ you are.
Lucy: Thanks. Can I ⁵ _____ them ⁶ _____ ?
Assistant: Yes, of ⁷ _____ .
Lucy: I think they're too big. Have you got a ⁸ _____ size?
Assistant: Yes, here's a thirty-seven.
Lucy: Great. I love them. I'll ⁹ _____ them.

7 Put the phrases in the correct order to make a dialogue.

Part 1
☐ James: I'm a size thirty-two.
☐ Assistant: Here you are, a size thirty-two.
☐ Assistant: What size are you?
☑ Assistant: Can I help you?
☐ James: I'm looking for a pair of jeans.

Part 2
☐ James: Yes, these are great, I'll take them.
☐ Assistant: Yes, of course.
☑ James: Can I try them on?
☐ Assistant: Yes, no problem, is a size thirty-four better?
☐ James: I think they are too small. Have you got a bigger size?

go green!

81

getting away

easy to do
a bit harder

Vocabulary

Visit Britain

1 Find the adjectives in the word square.
Look ➔ and ⬇.

> bad ✓   happy   busy   high   exciting
> good   hot   small   long   tall

b	a	d	e	t	p	r	s	e	r	h	p
h	a	p	p	y	t	o	i	m	m	i	f
s	t	t	d	p	i	e	c	c	t	g	h
h	h	i	e	i	f	s	t	u	e	h	i
h	b	u	s	y	n	n	s	s	d	d	g
g	a	e	x	c	i	t	i	n	g	a	h
o	u	b	e	n	r	a	t	l	p	t	r
o	h	f	p	p	h	t	l	l	r	l	e
d	t	t	t	y	o	i	e	l	l	l	l
e	f	n	r	n	t	t	n	e	h	m	o
k	c	m	e	d	h	v	m	i	e	e	n
m	t	a	l	l	a	s	m	a	l	l	g

2 Complete the sentences with the words below.

> mountain   Museum   River   university
> airport   roller coaster   castles ✓   pubs

1 Kings and Queens lived in _castles_ in the past.
2 I think the biggest _____ in London is
Heathrow. There are hundreds of flights.
3 I always visit the British _____ when I go
to London. There are a lot of interesting things
to see there and it's a beautiful building.
4 I think the highest _____ in the world
is Everest.
5 My dad loves the _____ in England.
He likes the traditional drinks.
6 I never go on the _____ when we go to
a theme park. I'm too scared!
7 We visited the _____ in Oxford where
many famous people studied.
8 London is on the _____ Thames. You can
take a boat trip on it.

Grammar

Superlative adjectives

3 ✱ Complete the text with the superlative
form of the adjectives in brackets.

Visit London, the ¹ _biggest_ (big) city in Britain.
There is so much to see and do.

- Take a trip up Canary Wharf tower, the
² _____ (tall) building in London, where
you can see the ³ _____ (beautiful) views
of the city. Travel along the ⁴ _____ (long)
underground transport system in the world.

- For culture you can spend a day at London's
Tate Modern art gallery – the ⁵ _____
(popular) gallery for tourists to visit – or go to
the ⁶ _____ (famous) tourist attraction
– Madame Tussauds. For shopping London is
fantastic – there are all kinds of shops in
Oxford Street, the ⁷ _____ (busy)
shopping street in Britain.

- There are also some very expensive shops,
where ⁸ _____ (rich) people in Britain
do their shopping.

- There is something for everyone in London –
⁹ _____ (exciting) city in the world!

4 ✱✱ Complete the sentences with the
superlative form of the adjectives below.

> hot   beautiful   old   expensive
> interesting ✓   tall

1 I love History. I think it is _the most
interesting_ subject that I study. It's fascinating.
2 I think Kate Winslet is _____
woman in the world.
3 _____ thing that I own is my
MP3 player, it cost over £100.
4 Tom is _____ boy in the class,
he's 1.80 metres!
5 My grandfather is eighty-nine, so he's
_____ person in my family.
6 I think Seville is _____ city in
Europe. It was forty-eight degrees last summer.

82

5 (✲✲) Use the prompts to make questions about the attractions. Use the superlative. Then answer the questions.

Tate Modern art gallery
Price: free
Opening times: 10 a.m.–10 p.m.
Visitors per year: 5 million
Facilities: gift shop, restaurant, café, and bar

Madame Tussauds
Price: £21.00
Opening times: 9 a.m.–6 p.m.
Visitors per year: 3 million
Facilities: gift shop

Tower of London
Price: £16.50
Opening times: 9 a.m.–5.30 p.m.
Visitors per year: 2 million
Facilities: gift shop, café

1 Which/expensive place?

Which is the most expensive place?
The most expensive place is Madame Tussauds.

2 Which is/cheap place?

_____ ?
_____ .

3 Which has/long opening times?

_____ ?
_____ .

4 Which is/popular?

_____ ?
_____ .

5 Which has/low number of visitors?

_____ ?
_____ .

6 Which has/good facilities?

_____ ?
_____ .

Grammar Plus: *less/the least*

6 (✲✲) Rewrite the sentences using *less* or *the least* and the adjective in brackets.

1 Football is the most boring sport. (interesting)
Football is the least interesting sport.

2 That café is the cheapest in town. (expensive)
_____ .

3 George is happier now. (sad)
_____ .

4 This is the easiest exercise. (difficult)
_____ .

5 I think Art is more interesting than PE. (boring)
_____ .

6 Canary Wharf is the ugliest building in London. (beautiful)
_____ .

Grammar reference

Superlative adjectives

Form

Adjectives	Comparatives	Superlatives
one syllable	add -*er*	add -*est*
old	old**er**	the old**est**
clean	clean**er**	the clean**est**
one syllable ending in -*e*	add -*r*	add -*st*
large	larg**er**	the larg**est**
nice	nic**er**	the nic**est**
one syllable ending in single vowel + single consonant	double the final consonant and add -*er*	double the final consonant and add -*est*
slim	slim**mer**	the slim**mest**
hot	hot**ter**	the hot**test**
one or two syllable ending in -*y*	change -*y* into -*ier*	change -*y* into -*iest*
dry	dr**ier**	the dr**iest**
happy	happ**ier**	the happ**iest**
two or more syllables	add *more* before the adjective	add *more* before the adjective
interesting	**more** interesting	the **most** interesting
dangerous	**more** dangerous	the **most** dangerous
irregular		
good	better	the best
bad	worse	the worst

Use

We use superlatives to compare people or things with all of the group to which they belong. We normally use *the* before a superlative.

*Who is **the most intelligent** student in your class?*
(the group = your class)
*Jessica is **the prettiest** girl I know.*
(the group = girls I know)
*This is **the most interesting** book in the library.*
(the group = the library)
*Your house is **the biggest** in our street.*
(the group = our street)

less and *the least*

Less and *the least* are the opposites of *more* and *the most*.

*Julia is **more** intelligent than Patricia.*
(= Patricia is **less** intelligent than Julia.)
*Your car is **more** expensive than mine.*
(= My car is less expensive than yours.)
*For me, Maths is **the most** interesting subject.*
*I don't agree, for me Maths is **the least** interesting subject.*

Vocabulary

Summer holidays

1 Put the words in the correct column.

> hotel   beach ✓   walking
> bed and breakfast   campsite
> camping   holiday apartment
> sightseeing   adventure

types of holiday	places to stay
beach	

2 Write the names of the types of holiday.

1 _beach_   2 _____

3 _____   4 _____

3 Match the people with the type of holiday in exercise 2.

1 Marta: I just want to relax and sunbathe.   _beach_

2 Jill: I want to learn new sports.   _____

3 Pete: I love visiting museums and galleries.   _____

4 Bill: I want to be in the countryside and get some exercise, but nothing very tiring.   _____

Grammar

be going to

4 (✳✳) Read Sophie's family's holiday 'to do' list and write sentences using *be going to*.

> **To do!**
> Before we go:
> book the campsite – dad
> clean the car – me
> buy the food – mum
> make sandwiches for the journey – Lily
> **on holiday**
> drive the car – mum
> put the tent up – dad and me
> cook the food – mum and Lily
> have fun – everyone!

Before we go:

1 Dad _is going to book the campsite._

2 I _____ .

3 Mum _____ .

4 Lily _____ .

On holiday:

5 Mum _____ .

6 Dad and me _____ .

7 Mum and Lily _____ .

8 Everyone _____ .

5 (✳✳) Write questions for Sophie with *be going to*.

1 go/France

  Are you going to go to France?

2 go/sightseeing

  _____ ?

3 cook/French food

  _____ ?

4 eat/in local restaurants

  _____ ?

5 swim/in the sea

  _____ ?

6 speak /French

  _____ ?

7 take/your school books

  _____ ?

8 sleep/in a tent

  _____ ?

6 (******) Complete the sentences with *be going to* and the verbs below.

> take   read ✓   finish   eat   not worry
> not swim ✓

1 I love reading so I <u>*am going to read*</u> lots of books.

2 Lily hates the water so she <u>*isn't going to swim in the sea*</u> .

3 We _____ lots of photos in Spain.

4 I don't know what kind of food we _____ on holiday.

5 Sarah _____ all her homework before she goes on holiday.

6 This year I _____ about exams.

7 (******) Complete the text about Tom's holiday plans with *be going to* and the verbs below.

> hang out   not speak   dance   eat
> not study ✓   speak

Tom is going on holiday next week with his family and some friends. They are going to France. Tom ¹ <u>*isn't going to study*</u> for his exams on holiday – he's going to have a good rest! He ² _____ at the disco with his friends and he ³ _____ on the beach. He ⁴ _____ much English – Tom learns French at school, so he ⁵ _____ French. He loves French food so he ⁶ _____ a lot!

8 (*****) Complete the dialogue using the correct form of *be going to* and the verbs in brackets.

Sophie: So what ¹ <u>*are you going to do*</u> (do) in the summer holidays, Sam?

Sam: We ² _____ (go) to Spain.

Sophie: Wow! ³ _____ (visit) Barcelona?

Sam: No, we ⁴ _____ (not/travel) to Barcelona, we ⁵ _____ (see) the Prado Museum in Madrid.

Sophie: Where ⁶ _____ (stay)? In a tent?

Sam: No, ⁷ _____ (not/camping) this year. I think ⁸ _____ (stay) in a bed and breakfast.

Grammar reference

be going to

Form

+	I **am** (**'m**) **going to** study He/She/It **is** (**'s**) **going to** study You/We/They **are** (**'re**) **going to** study	Music.
–	I **am not** (**'m not**) **going to** study He/She/It **is not** (**isn't**) **going to** study You/We/They **are not** (**aren't**) **going to** study	
?	**Am** I **going to** study **Is** he/she/it **going to** study **Are** you/we/they **going to** study	Music?
Short answers	Yes, I **am**. No, I'm not. Yes, he/she/it **is**. No, he/she/it **isn't**. Yes, you/we/they **are**. No, you/we/they **aren't**.	

Wh- questions	Answers
Where are you going to stay?	In a hotel.
What are you going to do?	Travel around Europe.
What time is Beth going to come home?	At about midnight.

Use

We use *be going to* to talk about future plans and intentions.

I**'m going to learn** Japanese next term.
They **aren't going to talk** to the teacher about it.
Are you **going to help** me tomorrow?

Vocabulary

Transport

1 Match the words below with the pictures.

> plane ✓   canoe   on foot   ship
> boat   helicopter

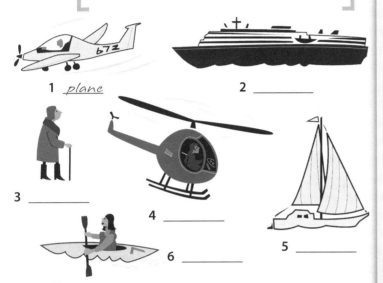

1 *plane*

2 _____

3 _____

4 _____

5 _____

6 _____

2 Complete the sentences with the words below.

> sail (x2)   skate   ride   fly   cycle
> drive   flew ✓

1 Last year I _*flew*_ in a helicopter for the first time.

2 I think only very rich people _____ yachts.

3 I'm going to learn to _____ because I have some inline skates.

4 1000 kilometres is too far to _____ a mountain bike.

5 You can't _____ your car into the city centre.

6 In England you can _____ a boat all the way around the island.

7 Sarah was too scared to _____ in a helicopter.

8 I have a mountain bike and I _____ to school everyday.

3 <u>Underline</u> the correct words to complete the sentence.

1 I don't like traffic, I prefer to go *on/go* foot.

2 You need a special licence to *drive/fly* a helicopter.

3 He went *by/on* canoe to Portugal.

4 I can't *drive/ride* a moped – I'm too young.

5 The ship *sailed/skated* to America in 1850.

6 Not many people know how to *ride/drive* a bus.

Reading

4 Look at the pictures. What do you know about these people? Read the text to check your ideas.

Amazing facts about the world's most famous TRAVELLERS and EXPLORERS!

Did you know that on Christopher Columbus's first journey there were just three small ships and around a hundred people working on the ship? The ships were smaller and slower than modern ships. Columbus sailed to the Canary Islands from Spain in five weeks. Today the same journey takes three or four hours!

Amelia Earhart was the first woman to fly across the Atlantic in 1932. She became one of the most famous women in the world after this journey. Sadly, Amelia disappeared in 1937 on her mission to fly around the world. The American government sent out soldiers to look for her. It was the most expensive rescue mission in history at the time but they didn't find her. She was forty years old.

Captain Scott explored Antarctica – Antarctica is one of the most enormous areas of land in the world (fifty times bigger than Britain) and possibly the coldest! He wanted to learn more about the weather and the plants in Antarctica. He became one of the most famous explorers in history.

Scott travelled mainly on foot, but on his second journey to the South Pole he took horses and dogs, too. The weather was not good – it became very stormy and windy and Scott didn't return. It is one of the saddest stories in history.

5 Read the text again and answer the questions.

1 How many ships sailed with Christopher Columbus on his first journey?

   a one   **b** two   **c** three

2 How long was Columbus's journey to the Canary Islands?

   a fifty-five weeks   **b** five weeks
   c four hours

3 Amelia Earhart was the first woman to:

   a sail across the Atlantic.
   b fly across the Antarctic.
   c fly across the Atlantic.

4 Amelia Earhart

   a flew around the world.
   b did not fly around the world.
   c flew across America.

5 Captain Scott went to the Antarctic to:

   a study the weather and plants.
   b become famous.   **c** study animals.

6 Captain Scott is

   a one of the saddest explorers in history.
   b one of the most famous explorers in history.
   c one of the biggest explorers in history.

6 Tick (✓) true or cross (✗) false.

1 ☐ There were a hundred ships on Columbus's first journey.

2 ☐ The ships were smaller than modern ships.

3 ☐ It took Columbus five hours to sail to the Canary Islands from Spain.

4 ☐ Amelia Earhart was forty years old when she flew across the Atlantic.

5 ☐ She became one of the most famous women in the world.

6 ☐ It cost a lot of money to try to find Amelia Earhart.

7 ☐ Britain is smaller than the Antarctic.

8 ☐ Scott travelled mainly with horses and dogs.

7 Answer the questions.

1 How many people travelled with Columbus on his first journey?

   _____ .

2 How long does it take a modern ship to sail from Spain to the Canary Islands?

   _____ .

3 What happened to Amelia Earhart in 1937?

   _____ .

4 What did Scott take on his second journey to the South Pole?

   _____ .

5 Why is Scott's second journey to Antarctica sad?

   _____ .

Listening

8 (18) Listen to the adverts and choose the correct answer.

1 Holiday 1 costs

   a £130.   **b** £1,300.   **c** £10,300.

2 Holiday 1 is to

   a Europe.   **b** America.
   c Europe and America.

3 Holiday 1 takes

   a two weeks.   **b** four weeks.
   c six weeks.

4 Holiday 2 takes

   a two weeks.   **b** three weeks.
   c six weeks.

5 What is the main form of transport for Holiday 2?

   a ship   **b** foot   **c** train

6 On Holiday 2 you sleep in

   a tents.   **b** local hotels.
   c bed and breakfasts.

7 Holiday 3 is in

   a the orient.   **b** Europe.   **c** America.

8 Holiday 3 costs

   a £15,000.   **b** £80.   **c** £800.

9 On which holidays do you travel to Europe?

   a holidays 1 and 2
   b holidays 1 and 3
   c holidays 1, 2 and 3

10 Which object is not talked about in the adverts?

   a camera   **b** walking boots
   c guidebook

9 (18) Listen again and tick (✓) the correct answer.

	Holiday 1	Holiday 2	Holiday 3
1 Which holiday is the most expensive?			
2 Which holiday is the longest?			
3 Which holiday is the shortest?			
4 Which holiday is the cheapest?			
5 Which holiday is the healthiest?			

self-assessment test 5

Vocabulary & Grammar

1 Choose the best word a, b or c to complete the sentences.

1 I don't like hotels. I prefer staying on a
   a camping.   b B&B.   c campsite. ✓

2 I always go to school on
   a bus.   b foot.   c motorbike.

3 There isn't any rain here. We have a lot of
   a droughts.   b hurricanes.   c floods.

4 I hate the sea, so I never travel by
   a ship.   b moped.   c helicopter.

5 I can't see much. It's very ___ today.
   a sunny   b windy   c foggy

6 My mum loves ___ . She always visits museums on holiday.
   a walking   b sightseeing   c camping

   /5

2 Match the words 1–7 from column A with the correct nouns a–g from column B.

A	B
1 solar	a boat
2 green	b skates
3 global	c spaces
4 pedal	d paper
5 holiday	e warming
6 recycled	f power
7 inline	g apartment

   /6

3 Complete the sentences with one word in each gap.

1 Do you usually choose products with little
   p _a_ _c_ _k_ _a_ _g_ _i_ _n_ _g_ ?

2 Do you recycle your r _ _ _ _ _ _ ?

3 I often go to the seaside. I love sitting on the
   b _ _ _ _ and relaxing in the sun.

4 P _ _ _ _ _ _ _ _ is a big problem in my city
   We've got a lot of traffic and very bad air.

5 We'll probably have heavy rain and s _ _ _ _ _
   tomorrow in the morning.

6 Our organisation 'Go Green' is for people who
   care about the e _ _ _ _ _ _ _ _ _ .

   /5

4 Complete the sentences with the comparative or superlative form of the adjective in brackets.

Robert has got three [1] _younger_ (young) sisters: Kate, Gina and Maria. Kate studies a lot and she's [2] _____ (good) student in her class. She is also [3] _____ (intelligent) than her sisters. Gina is very kind – in fact, she's [4] _____ (nice) person I know. Maria is very good-looking. She's certainly [5] _____ (tall) and [6] _____ (pretty) than the other two sisters. Many boys think she's [7] _____ (beautiful) girl in our school. But she can't play basketball very well – she's [8] _____ (bad) player on her team.

   /7

5 Complete the sentences with *going to* and the verbs in brackets.

1 Ian and Carol _are going to play_ (play)
   tennis at 6 p.m.

2 I _____ (not take) my camera.
   It's broken. Can you take yours?

3 Barbara has got a terrible toothache. She
   _____ (see) a dentist
   tomorrow morning.

4 _____ (you/help) me to do my
   Maths homework?

5 We have a History test on Monday. We
   _____ (study) hard this weekend.

   /4

6 Complete the sentences with the verbs below and the correct form of *will*.

> travel   not be   go up ✓   do

1 I think the price of petrol _will go up_ in the
   next five years.

2 In the future, people _____ most of their
   shopping on the Internet.

3 I hope there _____ any more natural
   disasters in the future.

4 Do you think people _____ to other
   planets in the next ten years?

   /3

Listening

7 (19) Listen to the conversation between two friends. Choose the best answer a, b or c.

1 Robert and his family are going to
  a go on a walking holiday.
  b do some sightseeing.
  c go camping.

2 When Jill went to France, her younger brother was ___ years old.
  a two   **b** three   **c** four

3 Jill wants to go on holiday with her
  a sister.   **b** boyfriend.   **c** parents.

4 Jill is going to
  a go bungee jumping again.
  b work in her father's shop.
  c ask her parents for money.

5 It's very ___ in the Alps at the moment.
  a cloudy   **b** windy   **c** rainy

/5

Reading

8 Read two students' answers to the question in a school newsletter. Tick (✓) true or cross (✗) false.

How Are You Helping To Save The World?

I don't do much for the environment but my mother really cares about it. She always tells us to turn off the lights and all electrical appliances when we are not using them. My sister is good at it but I still forget from time to time. Last week I forgot to turn off the taps in the bathroom and my mum was really angry. I think I need to change my habits.

Ann Roberts (Year 9)

I think my family and I are quite green. There's a lot of pollution in our area so we only use our car on rainy days. I often walk to school, my mother goes to work by bike and my father uses public transport. But we know it's not enough and we want to do more. Next week we're going to buy three bags – one for glass and metal, one for paper and cardboard and one for plastic. This way we will organise our rubbish better.

Paul Blackmoore (Year 7)

1 ☐ Ann is the greenest person in her family.
2 ☐ In Ann's family everybody saves water.
3 ☐ Ann needs to behave differently in the future.
4 ☐ Paul's father often cycles to work.
5 ☐ Paul and his family want to start recycling.

/5

Communication

9 Complete the dialogue with the words and phrases below. There are some extra words and phrases.

> have   help ✓   are   number   serve
> try   are they   looking for   size
> just looking   put   is it

Assistant: Can I ¹ _help_ you?
Sue: Yes, please. I'm ² _____ trainers.
Assistant: What ³ _____ are you?
Sue: Four, I think.
Assistant: OK. I've got a nice pair of trainers here. Here you ⁴ _____ .
Sue: Thanks. Can I ⁵ _____ them on?
Assistant: Of course.

Assistant: Everything OK?
Sue: Yes, thanks. How much ⁶ _____ ?
Assistant: £25.
Sue: I'll take them, please.

/5

10 Complete the dialogues with one word in each gap.

Dialogue 1
A: We're going to the disco. ¹H _ow_ about coming with us?
B: That's a ²g _____ idea!

Dialogue 2
A: We're going on a day out to Oxford. Why ³d _____ you come with us?
B: I'm sorry. I ⁴c _____ . I've got a test on Monday.

Dialogue 3
A: We're going to the cinema tomorrow. ⁵W _____ about coming with us?
B: OK, ⁶t _____ .

/5

Marks

Marks	
Vocabulary & Grammar	/30 marks
Listening	/5 marks
Reading	/5 marks
Communication	/10 marks
Total:	**/50 marks**

Vocabulary

Jobs

1 Match the activities 1–6 with the jobs a–f.

1 Take photos _b_
2 Work with children ___
3 Sell things ___
4 Work with animals ___
5 Talk on the phone ___
6 Look after people ___

2 Put the words below in the correct column.

> night   children   uniform   animals ✓
> money   the weekend

work with	wear	work at
animals		

3 Complete the sentences with the words below.

> sells   a uniform ✓   money   do
> phone   the weekend

1 I'm an actor so I don't wear _a uniform_ .
2 Most teachers don't work at _____ .
3 Bank clerks work with other people's
   _____ .
4 Do you think police officers talk on
   the _____ ?
5 A good shop assistant _____ lots
   of things.
6 Hairdressers _____ people's hair.

Grammar

have to

4 (*) Complete the answers to the questions with the short answers below.

> Yes, he does   Yes, she does
> No, they don't   No, I don't ✓
> No, you don't   Yes, they do

1 Do you have to get up early?
   No, I don't , I can get up when I want.
2 Do teachers have to wear a uniform?
   _____ , they wear their own clothes.
3 Does Sarah have to tidy her bedroom?
   _____ , every Saturday.
4 Do I have to go to school today?
   _____ , it's Sunday.
5 Do students have to pay?
   _____ , £6 each, please.
6 Does Pete have to go home now?
   _____ , his mother is waiting for him.

5 (*) Complete the sentences with *have to* or *don't have to*.

1 Hairdressers _don't have to_ sell things.
2 Vets _____ work with animals.
3 Office workers _____ work
   with children.
4 Photographers _____ take photos.
5 Teachers _____ wear a uniform.
6 Bus drivers _____ work with animals.

6 (**) John works in a café. Look at the list from John's boss and make sentences using *have to* or *don't have to*.

> John's tasks – Saturday
> wear your uniform ✓
> wash the floor ✗
> remember to be polite ✓
> close the shop at 5.30 ✓

1 _John has to wear his uniform_ .
2 _____ .
3 _____ .
4 _____ .

7 (✱✱) John phones the café manager to ask some questions. Use the prompts to complete the dialogue. Use *have to* or *don't have to*.

John: Hi Mr Dash.

Mr Dash: Hello John, is everything OK?

John: Yes, it's fine. I just have a couple of questions about the list you gave me.

Mr Dash: OK, no problem.

John: Well, firstly (I/open the café)
¹ *do I have to open the café?*

Mr Dash: Yes, you have to open the café at 9.30 a.m.

John: OK, and (I/tidy the café/before 9.00 a.m.)
² _____ ?

Mr Dash: Yes, that's right, and try and keep it tidy during the day.

John: (I/clean/windows) ³ _____ ?

Mr Dash: Oh no, you don't have to do that, John.

John: And what about the telephone, (I/answer phone)
⁴ _____ ?

Mr Dash: No, you don't.

John: Last question, (customers/pay with money)
⁵ _____ ?

Mr Dash: Customers can pay with credit card or cash. Is that everything?

John: Oh, just one last thing. (I/make cakes)
⁶ _____ ?

Mr Dash: No, you just have to sell them.

8 (✱✱) Complete Jason's email using *have to* or *don't have to* and a verb below.

> wash up   get up ✓   take   do   work   make
> clean   wear

✖

To: jason45@2gnmail.com
From: darren56@gemail34.com
Subject: New job

Hi Darren,

I've got a new job but I don't think I like it. I am looking after my aunt's children. They live in Oxford. She's got three small children and they are hard work! I ¹ *have to get up* early because the children sometimes get up at 6.00 a.m.! Then I ² _____ the breakfast and help the children to eat. I ³ _____ a uniform, I can wear what I like but the children make a lot of mess so I wear old clothes. After breakfast I ⁴ _____ the kitchen but I ⁵ _____ because my aunt has got a dishwasher. Then I ⁶ _____ the children to nursery school. That's the best part of the day, because I have a rest! But at the weekend I ⁷ _____ all day without a break. I'm glad this job is just for the summer and I ⁸ _____ it forever!

See you in September.

Jason.

have to

Form

+	I/You/We/They **have to work** / He/She/It **has to work**	on Saturday.
–	I/You/We/They **do not (don't) have to work** / He/She/It **does not (doesn't) have to work**	
?	**Do** I/you/we/they **have to work** / **Does** he/she/it **have to work**	on Saturday?

Short answers	Yes, I/you/we/they **do**. No, I/you/we/they **don't**. Yes, he/she/it **does**. No, he/she/it **doesn't**.

Wh- questions	Answers
What time do you have to get up?	At 6.30 a.m.
What do they have to do?	Answer customers' questions.
How many hours does she have to work?	Seven hours a day.

Use

We use *have to* to talk about obligation.

In England, children **have to wear** a uniform to school.

Sandra **doesn't have to go** to work on Monday.

Do we **have to write** this essay for tomorrow?

nice work?

Vocabulary

Feelings

1 Match the pictures to the feelings below.

[tired   sad   angry ✓   happy]

1 _angry_   2 _____   3 _____   4 _____

2 Underline the correct word in each sentence.

1 That wasn't an interesting lesson, I was very _bored/tired_.

2 Shirley was _excited/surprised_ she passed the exam, she thinks Maths is really difficult.

3 The children were all _tired/sad_ today because they went to bed very late last night.

4 My dad is _angry/nervous_ that I stayed out late. He has stopped my pocket money.

5 I always feel very _upset/nervous_ before a test.

6 I'm reading a really _sad/angry_ book.

7 I'm going on holiday next week!! I'm so _surprised/excited_.

8 Tara has lost her dog and she's very _angry/worried_ about it.

3 Complete the gaps with the words below.

[socialising   patient   skills   is   plays
humour   good at   memory   team ✓]

Let me tell you about my older brother James. Everyone thinks he's perfect! He is very independent. He does well at school and he likes working in a ¹ _team_ . He's ² _____ Maths and Science because he has a good ³ _____ . He's got lots of friends and is very good at ⁴ _____ . He's really popular because he ⁵ _____ polite and he has a good sense of ⁶ _____ . On Friday afternoons he ⁷ _____ the guitar in a band. But there is one thing he can't do – he doesn't have good computer ⁸ _____ . I always help him with his homework on the computer – he says that I'm great and very ⁹ _____ because we always spend one or two hours on the computer.

Grammar

Prepositions

4 (✳) Match phrases 1–6 with phrases a–f to make sentences.

1 My mobile phone is in

2 The teacher says we can't have mobile phones in

3 We're going to meet at

4 I always do my homework in

5 My dad comes home at

6 My birthday is on

a the living room.

b the same time every day.

c the cinema.

d my bag.

e Wednesday this year.

f class.

5 (✳) Underline the correct preposition to complete the text.

My boss Harry is a nice man but he can't get up ¹ _at/in_ the morning. We have to open the shop ² _at/in_ the same time everyday, so I usually have to do that. Our shop is an interesting place and I love working ³ _at/in_ the weekend because there are always lots of customers. It's not usually very busy ⁴ _in/at_ the week. He spends most of the day in his office and I don't think he often goes out ⁵ _in/on_ the evening but he says he is very happy.

6 (✳) Complete the gaps with _in_, _on_ or _at_.

1 There's a good programme _on_ TV tonight.

2 Jon has guitar lessons _____ Wednesday.

3 We eat lunch _____ the same time every day.

4 My birthday is _____ April.

5 School starts every day _____ 8.00a.m.

6 Bill can't get up _____ the morning.

Grammar Plus: *good at/bad at*

7 (✷✷) **Complete the sentences about Amy with** *good at* **or** *bad at*.

- – = quite good at   ✗ = bad at
- ✓ = good at   ✗✗ = very bad at
- ✓✓ = very good at

English lessons   ✓
play football   ✗✗
speak French   ✓✓
cook   ✗
surfing   –
remember people's names   ✗✗

1   *Amy is good at English lessons.*
2   _____ .
3   _____ .
4   _____ .
5   _____ .
6   _____ .

8 (✷✷) **Complete the gaps with the correct preposition.**

James,
Dentist appointment ¹ *on* Thursday
25 March ² ___ 6.00 ³ ___ the evening.
Don't forget and please try to be
more organised next time!

NEWTON COLLEGE
creative writing course!

Are you good at writing?
Come along to learn about writing ⁴ ___ a very
friendly class!

Course starts ⁵ ___ Monday evening
⁶ ___ 7.00 p.m. and then continues ⁷ ___ the
same time every week.

Vacancy for holiday representative

☆ Do you enjoy working ⁸ ___ the summer?
☆ We have some great jobs ⁹ ___ Europe!
☆ Are you reliable, polite and do you have
a good sense of humour?
☆ We want to hear from you!
☆ Fill in the application form and come to
one of our open days ¹⁰ ___ the
Greenfield School.

Grammar reference

Prepositions

Place

in my bedroom, **in** my house, **in** my bag

*The computer is **in** my bedroom.*
*My dog is **in** my house.*
*My keys are **in** my bag.*

on the bookshelf, **on** my desk

*The CDs are **on** the bookshelf.*
*Your books are **on** my desk.*

at the café, **at** the train station

*Jane is **at** the café with Sam.*
*We're **at** the train station.*

Time expressions

*at five o'clock, **at** half past ten*
at the same time
*in the morning, **in** the afternoon, **in** the evening, **at** night*
*on Monday, **on** Tuesday, **at** the weekend*
*in May, **in** April*
*on 1st May, **on** 27th April*

*Let's meet **at four o'clock** tomorrow.*
*I always have a shower **in the morning**.*
*What do you usually do **on Fridays**?*

> **Notice!**
>
> *My brother and I were born **in March**, I was born*
> *on **1st March** and he was born **on 26th March**.*

good at/bad at

- Use *good at/bad at* + *-ing* to talk about ability.

*Larry is **good at** skiing.*
*I'm **bad at** playing the guitar.*

- Use *not*, *quite* and *very* to modify the adjectives.

*We are quite **good at** playing tennis.*
*She isn't **bad at** singing.*

Listening

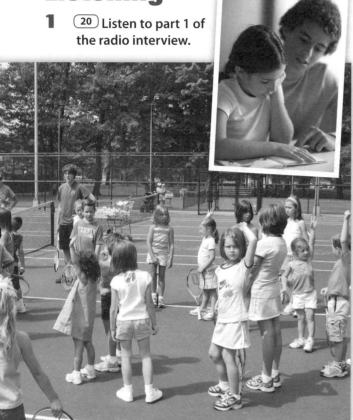

1 (20) **Listen to part 1 of the radio interview.**

1 What does Janek do?

2 What is special about the school?

2 (20) **Listen to part 1 again and complete the notes about Janek's school.**

Name of school: **Rainbow Bees**

Location: ¹ _____

School opens: ² _____

School closes ³ _____

Number of children at school: ⁴ _____

Age of children: ⁵ _____

3 (21) **Listen to part 2 and tick (✓) true or cross (X) false.**

1 ☐ Janek only drives the school bus in the morning.

2 ☐ There are ten volunteers at the school.

3 ☐ Janek helps to cook the lunches.

4 ☐ All the volunteers teach at the school.

5 ☐ All volunteers have to have experience of working with children.

6 ☐ Janek thinks volunteering at the school is an easy job.

7 ☐ Janek is going to college when the school closes.

8 ☐ Janek wants to be a driver.

Reading

4 **Read the text and put the tasks in the correct column.**

1 Have meals with the children

2 Listen to the children

3 Prepare the food

4 Tidy the bedrooms

5 Look after the children in their free time

6 Teach the children sport

7 Wash up

8 Serve the food

counsellor	activity leaders	kitchen and cleaning workers

5 **Read the text again and tick (✓) true or cross (X) false.**

1 ☐ For all the jobs you need to speak English well

2 ☐ Activity leaders help to prepare food.

3 ☐ Counsellors look after the children in their free time.

4 ☐ Kitchen workers have to get up early.

5 ☐ Activity leaders have to speak English well.

6 ☐ Kitchen workers have to be good at sport.

6 **Choose the correct answer.**

1 You don't need ___ to be a volunteer.

   a special training   **b** special clothes
   c special food

2 It's important to be good at ___ to be a counsellor.

   a sports   **b** listening   **c** Maths

3 The activity leaders teach

   a English.   **b** sport.   **c** cooking.

4 It's important that kitchen and cleaning workers like working

   a with people.   **b** alone.   **c** at night.

Do you want to make a difference to children's lives this summer?
Then volunteer for **Camp UK**!

Camp UK is a charity that organises summer camps for children with social problems or learning disabilities. Every year we need volunteers. You don't have to have any special training, you get free food and accommodation and a great experience. Here are some of the jobs that you can do.

Counseller

A counsellor takes care of a group of children. You have to look after the children in their free time, have meals with them and talk to the children about any problems they have.

Qualities needed: You have to have experience of working with children. Sometimes you have to work in your free time. You have to speak English very well.

Activity leaders

An activity leader helps the children to learn how to do a particular sport or activity. You teach the children how to do the activity safely and have fun.

Qualities needed: You have to be patient and good at communicating. You have to be good at sport and you have to have a good level of English.

Kitchen and cleaning workers

We need people to help prepare food and cook meals, serve the food and clean up after. We also need people to help keep the bedrooms and toilets clean and tidy.

Qualities needed: You have to get up early, so you have to be reliable and organised. You have to enjoy working in a team. You don't have to speak English well but you do have to have a good sense of humour!

Do you think you can help? Complete an application form today and help make a difference to young people's lives.

Writing

A formal letter

1 Write your address in the top right-hand corner: *77 Fleetwood Street, London*	Flat 5 77 Fleetwood Street Clapham London SW4 1BQ Tel: 020 765432

2 Write the name and address of the company you are writing to on the left: *Holiday Homes, King's café*

Hal's Holidays
112 Beesdale Road
Bristol
BS21 4HJ

3 Write the date under your address: *12 March 2010*

20 May 2010

Dear Ms France,

4 Open the letter with *Dear* + surname if you know the name or *Dear Sir* or *Madam* if you do not know the name.

I am writing to apply for the job of hotel receptionist. I saw the job advertisement on the 5th of May on the Holiday Help website.

5 Say why you are writing and use formal language: *I am writing to apply for, I would like to apply for …*

I have the necessary experience for the job. Last year I worked as a receptionist in a hotel in Paris for three months. I have got excellent people skills and I am very organised and reliable. I can speak French and Spanish fluently and I also speak basic German.

You can contact me by email on joolieG@hmail.com.

Yours sincerely,

Julie Granger

Julie Granger

6 Explain why you want or can do the job: (set each phrase on a different line) *I have sales experience, I worked in a hotel last year, I am reliable.*

7 Give contact details: *you can contact me by email …, please call me on …*

8 Close the letter with *Yours sincerely* when you start the letter with the person's name, or *Yours faithfully* when you start the letter with *Dear Sir* or *Madam*.

9 Sign your name.

10 Print your name.

1 Read the application letter and complete the sentences.

1 Julie lives in _____ .
2 She is applying for a job in _____ .
3 She is applying for the post of _____ .
4 Julie saw the advertisement on a _____ .
5 Last year Julie worked as a _____ in Paris.
6 She worked in Paris for _____ .
7 Julie is very _____ and _____ .
8 She can speak _____ , _____ and _____ .

2 Match the formal and informal phrases.

1 Write soon.
2 Take care.
3 Email me.
4 I would like to apply for the post of waitress.
5 I've done the job before.

a I want the job of waitress.
b Please contact me by email.
c I have the necessary experience for the job.
d Yours faithfully,
e I look forward to hearing from you.

3 a Underline the informal phrases in Luke's letter.

Hello Mr Green,

<u>I want to work</u> as a part time chef. My friend texted me about the job. She showed me the advertisement in the *Evening Herald*, on the 16th of May I think.

I can do the job no problem. I did it for two months last year in a hotel in central London. I was great because I'm very patient and I work hard, too.

Send me a text on my mobile – 798 2387654.

Speak soon.

Love,
Luke
Luke Lacker

b Rewrite the informal phrases using formal language.

I am writing to apply for the job of
part-time chef.

_____

_____

_____

_____

4 Complete the strategies box with the words below.

> Sign   sincerely   why   date ✓

A formal letter

- Include your address, the [1] *date* and the address of the company you are writing to.

- Explain where and when you saw the advertisement and [2] _____ you can do the job.

- Use formal language.

- Include contact details e.g. email or telephone number.

- Close the letter with *Yours* [3] _____ if you started with *Dear + surname*, or *Yours faithfully* if you started with *Dear Sir* or *Madam*.

- [4] _____ and print your name.

5 Read the task and then write your formal letter. Use the strategies in exercise 4 to help you.

> Write an application letter for the job advertisement below. Imagine you did a similar job last year in a gift shop in London.
> - Say why you are writing.
> - Say where you saw the job advertisement.
> - Describe your experience and skills.

DAILY RECORD   31 April

SITUATIONS VACANT

★ Are you friendly and reliable?

★ Do you enjoy working with people?

★ We are looking for a part-time sales assistant for this busy art shop.

★ Some sales experience needed.

Apply in writing to:
Patricia Guise, 13 Camden High Street, London.

Pat's Paints

Speaking

A job interview

6 Put the words in the correct order to make questions.

1 got/sales/any/experience/you/have
   Have you got any sales experience?

2 your/what/best/is/subject/at school
   _____?

3 you/from/where/are
   _____?

4 this/you/want/why/do/job
   _____?

5 languages/you/what/do/speak
   _____?

6 got/you/have/qualities/skills/what/and
   _____?

7 any/you/questions/have/got
   _____?

7 Match the questions 1–7 from exercise 6 with the answers a–g.

a [2] I think English is my best subject.

b [ ] Yes. How many people work for the company?

c [ ] Yes. I worked in a clothes shop for two years.

d [ ] I am very patient and organised.

e [ ] I like your products very much and I think this is a great place to work.

f [ ] I'm from Manchester, in the north of England.

g [ ] I can speak Italian and Spanish.

Vocabulary

Our world

1 Complete the crossword.

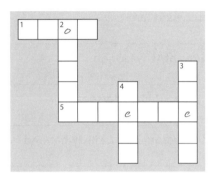

Across

1 B_____ your nose.

5 Re_____ a gift from someone.

Down

2 O_____ a gift to someone.

3 Bow to g_____ someone.

4 Have a m_____ .

2 Label the pictures with the phrases below.

> bow to greet   have a meal   offer a gift ✓
> receive a gift

1 *offer a gift*

2 _____

3 _____

4 _____

Grammar

if + imperative

3 ⸨*⸩ Match phrases 1–8 with phrases a–h to complete the sentences.

1 If you feel hot,   a cycle to school.

2 If you feel ill,   b read this book.

3 If you receive a gift,   c wear a sweater.

4 If you like detective   d call me.
   stories,

5 If you are cold,   e stay at home
                                and rest.

6 If you want to talk,   f ask the teacher.

7 If the traffic is bad,   g open the window.

8 If you don't know   h say 'thank you'.
   the answer,

4 ⸨*⸩ Underline the correct form to complete the sentences.

1 If you are cold, *close/don't* close the window.

2 *Learn/Don't learn* the grammar rules if you want to pass the exam.

3 If it is rainy, *don't forget/forget* your umbrella.

4 *Go/Don't go* outside if it is cold.

5 *Have/Don't have* a sandwich if you are hungry.

6 If you are tired, *sit/don't sit* down.

5 ⸨*⸩ Complete the sentences with the verbs below.

> go   like   call ✓   eat   get   take
> stay   forget

1 If the train is late, *call* me from the station.

2 Don't _____ on the bus if it's busy.

3 If Sarah calls, _____ a message.

4 If you _____ coffee, try the special cappuccino, it's delicious.

5 Visit your grandmother if you _____ to the village on Sunday.

6 If it's cold, _____ in the house.

7 If you are hungry, _____ the salad.

8 If you go out, don't _____ your coat.

6 (✱✱) Complete the sentences with the verbs in brackets.

1 If you _____ romantic stories, _____ this book. (like/read)
2 _____ to the cinema if you _____ homework to do. (not go/have)
3 If you _____ on holiday, _____ me a postcard! (go/send)
4 If you _____ fashion, _____ to this new clothes shop – it's fantastic! (like/go)
5 If you _____ to read at night, _____ the light on. (want/put)
6 If you _____ , please _____ me. (not understand/ask)

Grammar Plus: *if* and *when*

7 (✱) Complete the notes with the words below.

> have   leave   try   need   ask   says ✓
> understand   start ✓   turn   finish

EXAM RULES

1 When the teacher <u>*says*</u> 'start', <u>*start*</u> the test.
2 If you don't _____ the question, _____ the next one.
3 If you _____ more paper, _____ the teacher.
4 If you _____ a mobile phone, _____ it off.
5 If you _____ early, _____ the room quietly.

> wait   hear   see ✓   get   call   walk

HOTEL REX – fire alarms

● If you ⁶ <u>*see*</u> smoke, ⁷ _____ the fire brigade.
● If you ⁸ _____ the alarm, ⁹ _____ to the fire exit.
● When you ¹⁰ _____ outside, ¹¹ _____ with the other guests.

Grammar reference

if + imperative

Form

if + present simple +	imperative
If you *feel* cold,	*put on* a sweater.
If you *don't understand*,	*ask* the teacher to explain.
If you *have* a lot of homework,	*don't watch* TV.
If you *don't like* him,	*don't invite* him to your party.

Use

We use *if* + imperative to give somebody instructions or advice.

If you've got a pain in your knee, *go* to the doctor. (advice)
If you like her so much, *call* her and *ask* her out. (advice)
If you see John, *tell* him to come back to the classroom. (instructions)
If you don't know this word, *find* it in your dictionary. (instructions)

if/when + present simple, + imperative

We use *if* or *when* + present simple, + imperative to make a suggestion. The meaning of *if* and *when* here is the same.

If/When you feel cold, *put on* a sweater.
If/When you're thirsty, *drink* some water.
If/When you feel tired, *go* to bed early.

Vocabulary

Politics

1 Complete the crossword.

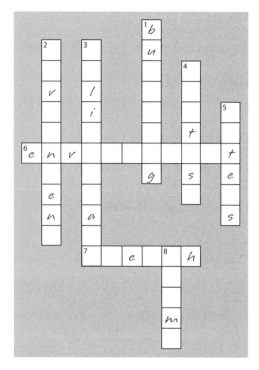

Across

6 The natural world.

7 When you talk in public you make a ___ .

Down

1 To hurt or frighten someone.

2 The organisation that controls the country.

3 People who work in politics.

4 We ___ about things we don't like.

5 People who vote in an election.

8 Does your town have a problem with knife ___ ?

2 Complete the text with the words below.

> environment   voters   protested
> elections ✓   crime   bullying   politics
> government

I always vote in MYP [1] _elections_ . I think it's important to vote. It helps find a solution to global problems like protecting the [2] _____ but also local problems like knife [3] _____ .
I am very interested in [4] _____ and last year I wrote to the [5] _____ . I [6] _____ about [7] _____ which is a big problem in my school.
It is important for politicians to know the opinions of young people because the students of today are the [8] _____ of tomorrow.

Grammar

Present perfect

3 (＊) Underline the correct word to complete the dialogue.

Journalist: Have you [1] <u>*spoken*</u>/*spoke* to all your voters?

Politician: No I [2] *have/haven't* but I have [3] *written/wrote* a letter to all the voters.

Journalist: Have you [4] *ever/never* made a speech?

Politician: Yes, of course I [5] *have/did* I have travelled all over the area and I have [6] *meet/met* a lot of people.

Journalist: I know you are also a good sports woman in your free time.

Politician: Yes, that's right. I have [7] *run/ran* two half marathons and I have [8] *swim/swum* a five kilometre race for charity.

Journalist: Wow, that's brilliant. [9] *Have/Did* you ever won any sporting competitions?

Politician: No, I have [10] *never/ever* won anything.

Journalist: Well, good luck in the election!

4 (＊＊) Put the words in the correct order to make sentences.

1 never/I/voted/have

   I have never voted.

2 organised/a protest/have/the students

   _____ .

3 haven't/we/a politician/met

   _____ .

4 have/you/read/book/this

   _____ ?

5 has/Kath/a car/never/driven

   _____ .

6 he/a speech/ever/has/made

   _____ ?

7 today/eaten/haven't/I/lunch

   _____ .

8 gone/students/the/have/home

   _____ .

5 (**) Read the notes the journalist has made for his interview with a politician and complete the sentences using the present perfect with *ever*.

1 organise/a protest?
2 make/a speech?
3 meet/any famous people?
4 visit/foreign countries?
5 speak to/the prime minister?
6 think about/changing your career?
7 protest about/climate change?
8 write to/voters?

1 *Have you ever organised a protest?*
2 _____ ?
3 _____ ?
4 _____ ?
5 _____ ?
6 _____ ?
7 _____ ?
8 _____ ?

6 (*) Complete the dialogue with the correct form of the present perfect.

Bill: ¹ *Have* you *been* (go) on holiday this year, Neil?

Neil: No, but I am going cycling in Italy in September. ² _____ you ever _____ (be) to Italy?

Bill: No, I ³ _____ . I ⁴ _____ always _____ (want) to go on a cycling holiday though.

Neil: Oh, why don't you come? I am going to Florence and then to a small town called Volterra. ⁵ _____ you _____ (hear) of it? They ⁶ _____ _____ (built) a new museum there and ⁷ _____ _____ (open) a new campsite. I think it will be a lot of fun.

Bill: Who are you going with?

Neil: I'm going with Mark from class 4C, ⁸ _____ you _____ (meet) him?

Bill: No, I don't think so but it sounds great.

Neil: ⁹ _____ you ever _____ (ride) a bike so far before?

Bill: No, but I can practise before we go.

Grammar reference

Present perfect

Form

+	I/You/We/They **have ('ve) met** He/She/It **has ('s) met**	a famous person.
–	I/You/We/They **have not (haven't) met** He/She/It **has not (hasn't) met**	
?	**Have** I/you/we/they **met** **Has** he/she/it **met**	a famous person?
Short answers	Yes, I/you/we/they **have**. No, I/you/we/they **haven't**. Yes, he/she/it **has**. No, he/she/it **hasn't**.	

Use

We use the present perfect to talk about experiences. We don't say when they happened.

I've won five swimming competitions.
He's voted in a lot of elections.

We often use *ever* in questions.

*Have you **ever** been to Africa?*
*Has she **ever** worked with children?*
*Have they **ever** swum in the sea in winter?*

We often use *never* in negative statements.

*I've **never** found any money in the street.*
*We've **never** run a marathon.*
*Barbara has **never** ridden a horse.*

> **Notice!**
>
> *My uncle **has climbed** Mont Blanc.* (present perfect)
>
> *He **climbed** it two years ago.* (past simple)

Listening

1 Look at the photos and the list of topics below.
What do you think the listening text will be about?

1 ☐ Weather	5 ☐ Shopping	9 ☐ Crime
2 ☐ Clothes	6 ☐ Language	10 ☐ Noise
3 ☐ Flats	7 ☐ People	11 ☐ Poverty
4 ☐ Food	8 ☐ Culture	12 ☐ Prices

2 (22) Listen to the conversation. Look at the apartments below.
Which one is the Mendez apartment?

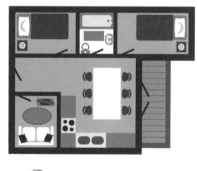

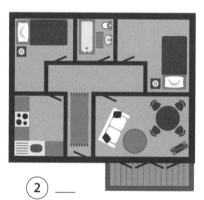

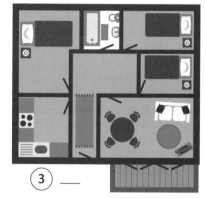

① __   ② __   ③ __

3 (22) Listen again and tick (✓) true or cross (✗) false.

1 ☐ The Varsy's thought the apartment in Seville was very big.
2 ☐ The Varsy's thought Seville was noisy.
3 ☐ They stayed outside the city.
4 ☐ They did a lot of sightseeing in Seville.
5 ☐ They cooked most of their own food.
6 ☐ They tried a lot of local food.
7 ☐ The weather was hot.
8 ☐ They spoke to local people in Spanish most of the time.

holiday home exchange blog ⊠

Home share shocks and surprises

Mr and Mrs Mendez from Seville tell us about their experience of home exchange. They exchanged their two bedroom flat in the centre of Seville for the Varsy's five bedroom house in the suburb of Redree in California for two weeks.

a ___

We have two children. Holidays cost a lot of money, so we have never travelled very far. On the Internet we found a 'home exchange' website. It was a good idea – we gave our home to an American family and we lived in their house for two weeks.

b ___

When we first arrived in Redree, California we thought the house was very big. There were five bedrooms and three bathrooms. The kitchen was the biggest room and the fridge was the size of a wardrobe! We were happy to have so much space to relax and a garden, too.

c ___

In Redree you have to drive everywhere, most people travel to work every day by car or bus. In Spain we usually walk everywhere. We live in the centre of town so this was very different for us.

d ___

In the evenings in Spain we usually go out late and we eat late, too – at about 9.30 p.m. We like to eat in bars and restaurants. The food in the restaurants in Redree was good and about the same price as in Spain but we discovered that many places closed at 10.00 p.m.

e ___

Everybody was very nice to us in Redree. The people in the shops and bars were very polite and helpful. It's a very quiet and relaxing place, and we really enjoyed our time there.

Reading

4 Read the text and match the titles 1–5 to the paragraphs a–e.

1 Transport
2 People and place
3 Food and entertainment
4 Before the holiday
5 The holiday home

5 Read the text again and choose the correct answer.

1 The Mendez family live in
  a a two bedroom house.
  b a five bedroom house.
  c a two bedroom flat.

2 They organised their holiday
  a on the Internet.
  b at the airport.
  c on the telephone.

3 The house they stayed in had
  a three bedrooms.
  b five bedrooms and a garden.
  c five bedrooms and no garden.

4 In America most people
  a walk to work.
  b drive everywhere.
  c take the bus everywhere.

5 In Spain the food is
  a better than the USA.
  b cheaper than the USA.
  c the same price as the USA.

6 In the USA
  a people don't eat in restaurants.
  b people prefer takeaway food in the evenings.
  c restaurants close earlier in the evenings.

6 Answer the questions.

1 How long were Mr and Mrs Mendez in the USA?

_____ .

2 Which was the biggest room in the Varsy's house?

_____ .

3 Why was the transport in the USA different for Mr and Mrs Mendez?

_____ .

4 What do the Mendez family usually do in the evening in Spain?

_____ .

5 How did Mr and Mrs Mendez describe the people in Redree?

_____ .

Reading

Matching

1 You are going to read an interview with a student who made a long trip by train. Read questions 1–3 and answer questions a–b.

1 Have you ever travelled 3,000 kilometres by train?
2 What do you like about travelling by train?
3 Why did you decide to go to Iran by train?

a Which question uses which tense?

Present simple: ____

Present perfect: ____

Past simple: ____

b <u>Underline</u> the question words in question 2 and 3.

2 Read the beginning of the interview. Match one of the questions 1–3 from exercise 1 with gap a.

3 Now read the rest of the interview and match questions 1–6 below with gaps b–f. There is one extra question.

1 Did you make any friends on the train?
2 Where did you stay in Tehran?
3 How long does the train journey take?
4 Was Tehran interesting?
5 What did you eat on the way?
6 Where are you going to travel next?

On the Trans Asia train

Today we interview Aleksander, a student from Warsaw, Poland, who travelled 2,968 kilometres from Istanbul to Tehran on the Trans Asia train.

a ___
Because it was cheaper than the plane and more comfortable than the bus. The ticket cost 53 Euros.

b ___
Three days. Well, 66 hours, to be exact. The train leaves Istanbul on Wednesday evening and arrives in Tehran on Saturday at 18.45.

c ___
I had water, orange juice, bread and some fruit.

d ___
Yes, I did. People on the train were very friendly. They offered me food and talked to me. Two young men spoke English. One of them, Reza, later showed me Tehran.

e ___
Yes, it was. It's a big, very polluted city but the parks are beautiful. People put carpets on the grass and sit there and drink tea. There are also mountains around the city. And I met some fantastic people.

f ___
Right now I'm going to study. And next summer I'm going to cycle around the Baltic sea.

Listening

Note-taking

4 Read the listening task in exercise 5. Match the groups of possible answers a–e with the gaps 1–5.

a style/colour/price
b red/green/blue
c Monday/Tuesday/Friday
d 11 a.m./5 p.m./7 p.m.
e 30/45/60

5 (23) Listen to the manager of a clothes shop talking to some new shop assistants. Complete the gaps with the missing information.

Sapphire Fashions	*Shop assistants' duties*

Working hours: from 10 a.m. to ¹_____

Lunch break: ²_____ minutes

If you work on Saturday, you don't have to work on ³_____

Uniform: black shirt, black trousers and a ⁴_____ scarf

Help customers find the right size and ⁵_____

Use of English

Gap fill

6 Choose the correct answer a, b or c for each gap.

1 Kevin _b_ never been to Spain.

   a have   **b** has   **c** is

2 I'm going to Paris ___ Thursday.

   a in   **b** at   **c** on

3 Jenny and Tom ___ tennis every Saturday.

   a play   **b** plays   **c** playing

4 Andy is ___ travel round the world next year.

   a will   **b** have to   **c** going to

5 I wanted to go to Greece ___ I didn't have enough money.

   a and   **b** but   **c** so

7 What did you have to do in each sentence in exercise 6? Match explanations a–e with sentences 1–5 in exercise 6.

   a Choose the right preposition.   _2_

   b Choose the right linking word.   ___

   c Choose the correct present tense form.   ___

   d Complete a verb in the present perfect.   ___

   e Choose the right verb form to talk about a future intention.   ___

Exam TIP

The type of task tests some of the grammar you have learned. Try to remember the rules.

8 Choose the correct answer a, b or c for each gap.

What's more important?

I have never [1] _b_ voluntary work. I haven't got much time. I have to study really hard because I want to go to a good university. My friend Cathy is different. She's not very good [2] ___ school subjects but she does a lot of other things. She [3] ___ in a band on Tuesdays and looks after disabled children on Fridays. Last Friday I went with her. Cathy is very patient [4] ___ the children love her. I helped [5] ___ a bit. It was not easy but I felt happy. In the evening I made a decision. I'm [6] ___ some voluntary work, too.

1 **a** did   **b** done   **c** doing

2 **a** in   **b** on   **c** at

3 **a** is singing   **b** sings   **c** has sung

4 **a** and   **b** but   **c** because

5 **a** him   **b** she   **c** her

6 **a** doing   **b** done   **c** going to do

Speaking

Making suggestions and responding

9 Read the oral exam task and put the conversation below in order.

Imagine the following situation. You and your friend want to buy a present for your friend Emily's birthday. She's got a very 'green' lifestyle. Look at the pictures of presents and decide together which present you are going to buy.

Save the Rainforests

100% recycled paper

a ☐ I agree, they are fun and better for the environment than cars. But they are the most expensive thing here. We haven't got a lot of money. What about the T-shirt?

b ☐ I'm not sure. It's nice, but I think Emily wears a smaller size.

c ☐ You're right, she does. So what are we going to buy? The notebook? It's pretty, but it's the cheapest gift of all!

d ☑ 1 OK, what have we got here? A T-shirt, a notebook and inline skates. What do you think? The inline skates are great.

e ☐ OK. We'll take five notebooks.

f ☐ So let's buy five of them with different pictures. She likes notebooks.

Vocabulary & Grammar

1 **Complete the job definitions with one word in each gap.**

1 An a _ctor_ acts in a play or in a film.
2 A v_____ works with animals.
3 A bank c_____ works with money.
4 A n_____ helps people in hospital.
5 A p_____ takes photos of people and places.
6 A shop a_____ sells things in a shop.

/5

2 <u>Underline</u> **the correct word to complete the sentences.**

1 I didn't know you're good at tennis. I'm really _surprised/worried_.
2 Ella always says 'please' and 'thank you'. She's very _polite/organised_.
3 I'm really _nervous/bored_. There's nothing to do.
4 Tom always forgets about our meetings. He isn't very _reliable/confident_.
5 The teacher was very _tired/angry_ because a lot of students didn't do their homework.
6 My mum always makes time to help me with my homework. She's very i_ndependent/patient_.

/5

3 **Complete the sentences with the present perfect. Use all the words in brackets and one verb below.**

> vote   organise   receive   meet
> have ✓   make   drive

1 Have _you ever had_ (you/ever) a meal in a very expensive restaurant?
2 We _____ (never) a famous politician.
3 _____ (they/ever) in an election?
4 I _____ (never) a speech in public.
5 _____ (Barbara/ever) a very expensive gift?
6 _____ (you/ever) a special event in your school?
7 My sister _____ (never) a car.

/6

4 **One preposition in each sentence is wrong. Find it and correct it.**

1 I usually go out with my friends at the evening.
   in the evening
2 Tom is bad with remembering names but at the same time he remembers faces very well.
   _____
3 Bethany was born in 12 March.
   _____
4 Robert is going to meet Charlie on the cinema.
   _____
5 Last Sunday I got up on 11 o'clock.
   _____
6 Eating healthy food is good for you so I'm going to buy some healthy food in Saturday.
   _____

/5

5 **Write positive sentences (+), negative sentences (–) or questions (?). Use the verbs in brackets and the correct form of _have to_.**

1 I _have to wear_ (wear) a uniform to school. (+)
2 _____ (your father/work) at night. (?)
3 We _____ (go) to school tomorrow. It's Saturday. (–)
4 Sandra _____ (do) her homework on the computer. (+)
5 _____ (you/be) there very early. (?)
6 Sam _____ (tidy) his room. (–)

/5

6 **Put the words in the correct order to make sentences with _if_ + imperative.**

1 have/the dentist/go to/you/toothache,/If
   If you have toothache, go to the dentist.
2 bored,/this programme/If/are/you/watch
   _____ .
3 relax,/long bath/want to/you/If/a/take
   _____ .
4 early/you/go to bed/feel tired,/If
   _____ .
5 don't forget/Joe's birthday party,/go to/the present/you/If
   _____ .

/4

106

Reading

7 Read the article. Choose the best option, a, b or c to complete the gaps in the text.

HOW TO LEARN ABOUT OTHER CULTURES

There are a lot of ways to experience other cultures.

1 ___ . You can travel via the internet and learn about other countries without ever leaving your house!

>>> TIPS >>>

2 ___ . Reading through travel books and travel journals gives you great ideas about local and international destinations.

Take a class at your community college that helps you learn about another culture. **3** ___ . It can be a dance class, like capoeira from Brazil, or a cooking class, like learning how to make mole from Mexico.

4 ___ . You can do it in many ways: read newspapers from other countries online, browse local websites with information about entertainment, trips and trends. Or take a look at local forums and blogs to get into real everyday slang and culture.

If you still want to travel, investigate exchange programmes in your community. Many cities have 'sister city' exchange programmes which select young people to visit the town's sister city for a week.

Remember it is always good to have a friend from another culture. **5** ___ .

1 a They go on a long trip around the world and visit many countries.
  b You don't have to take a long plane flight and spend lots of money.
  c Some people have never travelled to other countries by plane.

2 a Visit the library to find travel books.
  b Don't travel without a good book and a newspaper.
  c Buy a good book at your international destination.

3 a Dancing classes are very interesting.
  b Learn how to cook Mexican dishes.
  c It doesn't have to be a language class.

4 a Start writing a blog.
  b Book your trip online.
  c Explore the Internet.

5 a It helps you learn more about how people act and think.
  b Many of my friends have never had a friend from another culture.
  c You don't have to communicate with your friends by email.

/5

Listening

8 (24) Listen to the interview with three people. Answer the questions with their names: Alicia (A), Paul (P) or Hannah (H).

Who:

1 has to be good at languages? ____
2 had a job as a shop assistant? ____
3 is new in her job? ____
4 is looking for a job now? ____
5 feels bored at work? ____
6 has to get up quite early? ____
7 finishes work early in the afternoon? ____
8 likes his/her job the best? ____

/8

Communication

9 Use the words in brackets to write questions for the answers at a job interview. The interview is for an English teacher at a summer school.

1 _What's your name_ ? (name)
  My name is Steven Jones.

2 _____ ? (from)
  I'm from Denver, Colorado.

3 _____ ? (languages)
  I speak English and a little bit of Spanish.

4 _____ ? (subject)
  I'm very good at Maths and English.

5 _____ ? (experience)
  Yes, I have. Last year I worked with a group of children. I helped them with their Maths and English.

6 _____ ? (qualities)
  I'm very reliable. I like working with children and I have a good sense of humour.

7 _____ ? (want)
  I want to have more experience of working with children. And I need a summer job.

8 _____ ? (questions)

/7

Marks

Vocabulary & Grammar	**/30 marks**
Reading	**/5 marks**
Listening	**/8 marks**
Communication	**/7 marks**
Total:	**/50 marks**

exam test 1

Reading

To: dave@1gemail.com
From: pav@gemail67.com
Subject: Hello from Edinburgh!

Hi Dave,

I hope you're OK. I'm here in Edinburgh. It's great. There are a lot of things to do. I like the school, too. The teacher is really nice. She speaks very clearly, so I can understand her easily. People in the shops and in the street are more difficult to understand.

I've got two new friends: Miguel and Roberta. Miguel is from Brazil. We play football after school. He can play really well. His three brothers in Brazil are also brilliant footballers.

Roberta is Italian. She's very pretty and she likes Art. We often go to museums. There are a lot of museums in Edinburgh. We also study and have lunch together.

In the evenings there are often parties for all the students. We dance and have fun. Sometimes Miguel plays the guitar.

I'd like to see you. I can come to York for the weekend. Is that OK?

See you soon,
Pavel

1 Read Pavel's email to his English friend. Tick (✓) true or cross (✗) false.

1 ☐ Pavel goes to school in Edinburgh.
2 ☐ Pavel can understand all the people in the streets easily.
3 ☐ Miguel and his brothers are good football players.
4 ☐ Roberta is only interested in Italian art.
5 ☐ There is a party for students every evening.
6 ☐ Pavel wants to meet Dave in York.

/6

Listening

2 (25) Listen to four short recordings. Choose the best answer a, b or c.

1 When is Debbie's birthday?
  a 3 April   **b** 6 April   **c** 13 April

2 What do they decide to do after school?
  a    **b**   **c**

3 Where is the cat?
  a   **b**   **c**

4 Where are the people?
  a A bookshop.   **b** A police station.   **c** A school.

/4

Use of English

3 Read the text. Complete the text with a word below. There is one extra word.

does   go   goes
her ✓   out   plays
their   there   to
up   usually
watches

Different interests

Laura and ¹ *her* sister Sarah have got very different interests. Laura likes sports. ² _____ is a big sports centre near their house. On Saturdays she ³ _____ tennis there after breakfast. Sarah ⁴ _____ shopping with her friends. After lunch Laura usually meets her boyfriend Tom. They do sports or listen ⁵ _____ music. Sarah hangs ⁶ _____ with friends at a café. Both sisters have dinner with ⁷ _____ parents. In the evening Laura and Tom ⁸ _____ dancing and Sarah ⁹ _____ TV. On Sunday morning Laura ¹⁰ _____ her homework. Sarah ¹¹ _____ talks on the phone. So, which sister is like you?

/10

Marks	
Reading	/6 marks
Listening	/4 marks
Use of English	/10 marks
Total:	**/20 marks**

exam test 2

A special day in my life

The winner of our essay competition is Millie Leigh from Worthing. Millie, 16, wrote about her tenth birthday.

I remember my tenth birthday very well. I got a lot of cards. There was a card in French from my aunt in France. And my sister made a special card with photos of the whole family.

In the morning I put decorations in all the rooms and lights in the garden. Dad cooked a delicious meal and Mum made a birthday cake with candles.

I changed my clothes three times that day. In the morning I wore jeans and a T-shirt. Then I put on a new dress for the party. But it got dirty before everyone arrived so in the end I wore a skirt and a sweater.

In the evening, my grandparents, my aunt and uncle and my three cousins arrived. I got just one present but what a present! It was my first computer. My dream! It was fantastic!

After dinner, my sister, my cousins and I played in the garden. Then we played computer games on my new computer. We sent lots of emails to friends. When it was dark, we had fireworks in the garden. I went to bed very late and very happy. ""

Reading

1 **Read the story. Then choose the best answer a, b or c for the questions.**

1 What did Millie's sister make for her birthday?
  a She wrote a card in a foreign language.
  b She created a card with pictures.
  c She made a birthday cake.

2 What did Millie do in the morning?
  a She made a birthday cake.
  b She decorated the house.
  c She put decorations in the garden.

3 What did Millie wear for her birthday party?
  a A skirt and a sweater.
  b Jeans and a T-shirt.   c A new dress.

4 Why did Millie like her present?
  a It was useful.   b It was expensive.
  c She wanted one very much.

5 What did the children do at the party?
  a They used the new computer to chat to friends.
  b They played sports in the garden.
  c They did a lot of fun activities.

/5

Listening

2 **(26) Listen to the conversation between Lucy and Sam. Tick (✓) true and cross (✗) false.**

1 ☐ Sam and Lucy want to cook something for lunch.

2 ☐ Lucy doesn't eat meat.

3 ☐ They haven't got any olives.

4 ☐ The big bowl is in the cupboard.

5 ☐ There aren't any lemons.

/5

Use of English

3 **Put the words in the correct order to make sentences.**

1 Nicola Tesla/what/invent/did
  What *did Nicola Tesla invent?*

2 salad/the/am/mixing/I
  I _____ .

3 favourite/what/food/your/is
  What _____ ?

4 is/hat/she/a/wearing/not
  She _____ .

5 go/did/party/where/he/after/the
  Where _____ ?

6 Internet/the/live/we/changed/way/the
  The _____ .

7 people/at/you/meet/did/new/many/festival/the
  Did _____ ?

8 enjoy/tent/don't/in/a/I/sleeping
  I _____ .

9 have/I/to/return/a/ticket/Manchester/can
  Can _____ ?

10 New/you/how/the/celebrate/did/Year?
  How _____ ?

11 finished/have/I/my/homework
  I _____ .

/10

Marks
Reading	/5 marks
Listening	/5 marks
Use of English	/10 marks
Total:	/20 marks

exam test 3

Reading

1 Read the interview with a London taxi driver. Match questions a–f with gaps 1–5. There is one extra question.

1 ___

Yes, it was. I had to pass a difficult exam. London taxi drivers have to know all the streets in central London and all the important buildings, such as government offices, hotels and museums.

2 ___

It's working with people and I like talking to them. Most passengers are friendly and polite. Another good thing is that I can work when I want.

3 ___

I don't have to but I often do. The money is better … and the work is interesting. But I'm very tired in the morning.

4 ___

Yes, I have. I have driven politicians, actors, sports people. I once drove the actress Kate Winslet from the airport to her hotel. She was very nice to me.

5 ___

No, in a few years I'm going to start my own transport company.

a Are you going to be a taxi driver all your life?
b Do you have to work at night?
c Have you ever driven someone famous?
d What did you have to do to become a taxi driver?
e Was it difficult to get a job as a taxi driver?
f What's the best thing about being a taxi driver?

| /5 |

Listening

2 (27) You are going to hear a teacher talking to a group of students on a school trip. Complete the missing information.

Year 12 class trip to Italy – Day 3

Leave at: 8.15   Arrive in Bologna at ^{1} _____

Activities in Bologna: ^{2} _____ (three hours):
university, museum, churches

Lunch at 2 p.m.   Drive to Rimini

Staying at a ^{3} _____ in Rimini

Day 4

Morning: on the ^{4} _____ in Rimini

Teacher's phone number: ^{5} _____

| /5 |

Use of English

3 Read Tricia's email to Jane. Choose the best answer a, b or c to the questions.

To: jane@1gimail2.com
From: tricia@gemail34.com
Subject: Holiday

Hi Jane,

Guess what – I've got a holiday job at a café. I started ^{1} _b_ Monday. The beginning was a bit difficult. I made some mistakes ^{2} ___ the boss was very patient. Now I make the coffee and serve it and wash the cups and work ^{3} ___ money – I do everything. A lot of tourists come to the café and sometimes I ^{4} ___ speak French or Spanish. The customers are happy when they hear I ^{5} ___ speak their language. I finish ^{6} ___ 11 p.m. I ^{7} ___ never worked so late! I'm really tired ^{8} ___ the evening but I like it here. It's ^{9} ___ than the job at the supermarket I had last summer. I'm going ^{10} ___ for four weeks and then I'm going on a walking holiday in Scotland with Dave. We ^{11} ___ to walk up Ben Nevis this year. What about you?

Love,
Tricia

1	a in	b on ✓	c at
2	a so	b because	c but
3	a in	b with	c for
4	a can	b have to	c did
5	a can	b have to	c will
6	a in	b on	c at
7	a has	b have	c was
8	a in	b on	c at
9	a better	b best	c more good
10	a working	b work	c to work
11	a is going	b are going	c will

| /10 |

Marks

Reading	/5 marks
Listening	/5 marks
Use of English	/10 marks
Total:	/20 marks

people

appearance

attractive (adj)
beard (n)
beautiful (adj)
dark (adj)
fair (adj)
friendly (adj)
fun (adj)
glasses (n)
good-looking (adj)
hair (n)
long (adj)
moustache (n)
nice (adj)
pretty (adj)
short (adj)
shy (adj)
slim (adj)
strong (adj)
tall (adj)
young (adj)

clothes and accessories

accessories (n)
baseball cap (n)
belt (n)
boots(n)
casual (adj)
clothes (n)
dress (n)
earrings (n)
fashion (n)
fashionable (adj)
hat (n)
hoodie (n)
jacket (n)
jeans (n)
piercing (n)
scarf (n)
school uniform (n)
shirt (n)

shoes (n)
skirt (n)
sweater (n)
tie (n)
tracksuit (n)
trainers (n)
trousers (n)
T-shirt (n)
wellies (n)

feelings and emotions

angry (adj)
bored (adj)
happy (adj)
sad (adj)
surprised (adj)
tired (adj)
upset (adj)
worried (adj)

nationality

American (adj)
Argentinian (adj)
Brazilian (adj)
British (adj)
Hungarian (adj)
Irish (adj)
Italian (adj)
Mexican (adj)
Polish (adj)
Scottish (adj)
Spanish (adj)
Turkish (adj)

personal character

be good at sports/Maths/
playing the guitar (v)
have a good memory (v)
have a good sense of humour (v)
identity (n)
independent (adj)
nervous (adj)
nickname (n)
organised (adj)

patient (adj)
personality (n)
polite (adj)
qualities (n)
reliable (adj)
sense of humour (n)
sociable (adj)
student (n)
successful (adj)
teenager (n)

personal information

age (n)
email address (n)
name (n)
nationality (n)
phone number (n)

possessions

bicycle (n)
boyfriend (n)
brush (v)
camera (n)
CD (n)
chewing gum (n)
chocolate (n)
computer (n)
diary (n)
DVD player (n)
earphones (n)
friend (n)
games console (n)
girlfriend (n)
guitar (n)
hairbrush (n)
ID card (n)
inhaler (n)
jewellery (n)
keys (n)
lamp (n)
lip salve (n)
magazine (n)
make-up (n)
mirror (n)

mobile phone (n)
MP3 player (n)
packet (n)
perfume (n)
pet (n)
purse (n)
skateboard (n)
sunglasses (n)
tissues (n)
TV (n)
umbrella (n)
wallet (n)

house

furniture
armchair (n)
basin (n)
bath (n)
bathtub (n)
bed (n)
bookshelf (n)
bowl (n)
carpet (n)
chair (n)
cooker (n)
cupboard (n)
dishwasher (n)
fridge (n)
furniture (n)
live (v)
sink (n)
sofa (n)
table (n)
taps (bathroom) (n)
teapot (n)
toilet (n)
TV (n)
wardrobe (n)
washing machine (n)

rooms
bathroom (n)
bedroom (n)
flat (n)
garden (n)
house (n)

kitchen (n)
living room (n)
room (n)

school

classroom objects
bookcase (n)
calculator (n)
computer (n)
desk (n)
dictionary (n)
eraser (n)
interactive whiteboard (n)
pen (n)
pencil (n)
pencil case (n)
pencil sharpener (n)
poster (n)
ruler (n)
scissors (n)

school life
break (n)
canteen (n)
class (of students) (n)
classmate (n)
clean (v)
evening class(n)
exam (n)
exercise book (n)
fail (v)
goal (aim) (n)
homework (n)
lesson (n)
library (n)
mate (n)
pass (an exam) (v)
teacher (n)
tidy the classroom (v)
walk to school (v)
wear school uniform (v)

school subjects
Design and Technology (n)
English (n)
Foreign languages (n)
Geography (n)

History (n)
ICT (Information and Communication Technology) (n)
Maths (n)
Music (n)
PE (n)
Science (n)

work

job tasks
answer (v)
company (business) (n)
customer service (n)
cut people's hair (v)
hard-working (adj)
have good computer skills (v)
interview (n)
look after people (v)
sell things (v)
speak clearly (v)
take photos (v)
talk on the phone (v)
type (v)
wear a uniform (v)
work at night/the weekend (v)
work with animals/children/
money (v)

jobs
babysitting (v)
bank clerk (n)
builder (n)
bus driver (n)
car mechanic (n)
cook (job) (n)
dentist (n)
doctor (n)
earn (money) (v)
electrician (n)
engineer (n)
experience (of working in sales) (n)
hairdresser (n)
job (n)
journalist (n)
lawyer (n)
nurse (n)
office worker (n)

part-time job (n)

photographer (n)

plumber (n)

police officer (n)

postman/postwoman (n)

scientist (n)

shop assistant (n)

skill (n)

teacher (n)

vet (n)

volunteer (v)(n)

waiter (n)

family and social life

daily routine

commuter (adj)

cycle to school (v)

daily (adj)

do homework (v)

finish (v)

get dressed (v)

get up (v)

go by bus (v)

go home (v)

go to bed (v)

go to school (v)

go to sleep (v)

have a shower (v)

have breakfast (v)

have dinner (v)

have lunch (v)

home (n)

play football (v)

start (v)

study (v)

talk (v)

talk with friends (v)

wake up (v)

watch TV (v)

family members

aunt (n)

brother (n)

child (n)

children (n)

cousin (n)

Dad (n)

daughter (n)

father (n)

Gran (n)

Granddad (n)

grandfather (n)

grandmother (n)

grandparents (n)

husband (n)

mother (n)

Mum (n)

parents (n)

relatives (n)

sister (n)

son (n)

uncle (n)

wife (n)

holidays and festivals

birthday (n)

candles (n)

cards (n)

celebrate (v)

celebration (n)

costume (n)

decorate (v)

fireworks (n)

hold hands (v)

New Year (n)

New Year's Day (n)

New Year's Eve (n)

parade (n)

party (n)

present (n)

special clothes (n)

special food (n)

street party (n)

sweets (n)

traditional dancing (n)

leisure time

channel (n)

computer games (n)

dancing (n)

guest(n)

hang out (v)

juggle (v)

lifestyle (n)

relax (v)

roller coaster (n)

theme park (n)

food

apples (n)

bacon (n)

banana (n)

biscuits (n)

bread (n)

broccoli (n)

cake (n)

carrot cake (n)

carrots (n)

cereal (n)

cheese (n)

coffee (n)

crisps (n)

croissant (n)

dessert (n)

drink (n)

eggs (n)

fish (n)

food (n)

fresh (adj)

fruit (n)

grapes (n)

green bean (n)

ham (n)

hamburger (n)

hot chocolate (n)

ice-cream (n)

juice (n)

junk food (n)

lemon (n)

lemonade (n)

lettuce (n)

mayonnaise (n)

meat (n)

milk (n)

mineral water (n)

muffin (n)

mushrooms (n)

nut (n)

oil (n)

olive (n)

onions (n)

oranges (n)

paella (n)

pasta (n)

pears (n)

peas (n)

pie (n)

pizzas (n)

potatoes (n)

ready meal (n)

rice (n)

roast chicken (n)

salad (n)

sandwich (n)

snack (n)

takeaway food (n)

tea (n)

toast (n)

tomatoes (n)

tuna (n)

vegetables (n)

water (n)

meals
breakfast (n)

foreign food (n)

lunch (n)

make breakfast (v)

traditional dish (n)

preparing food
boil (v)

cooking (v)

cut (v)

ingredients (n)

mix (v)

put (v)

recipe (n)

talking about food
chew (v)

delicious (adj)

hungry (adj)

vegetarian (n)

shopping and services

places in town
art gallery (n)

bridge (n)

café (n)

car park (n)

cinema (n)

club (n)

department store (n)

fire station (n)

hospital (n)

hotel (n)

library (n)

market (n)

museum (n)

opera house (n)

park (n)

police station (n)

post office (n)

restaurant (n)

school (n)

shopping mall (n)

sports centre (n)

stadium (n)

swimming pool (n)

town centre (n)

town hall (n)

underground railway (n)

university (n)

shopping
cheap (adj)

checkout (n)

price (n)

shampoo (n)

size (n)

try on (v)

shops
clothes shop (n)

greengrocer's (n)

music shop (n)

newsagent's (n)

pharmacy (n)

shoe shop (n)

sports shop (n)

stationery shop (n)

supermarket (n)

travelling and tourism

holidays
adventure (n)

beach (n)

bed and breakfast (B&B) (n)

boring (adj)

camping (n)

campsite (n)

cheap (adj)

exciting (adj)

expensive (adj)

foreign (adj)

go sightseeing (v)

holiday apartment (n)

hotel (n)

interesting (adj)

map (n)

tent (n)

tourist (n)

walking (n)

transport
aeroplane (n)

airport (n)

boat (n)

(by) air (n)

(by) land (n)

(by) sea (n)

bus (n)

canoe/kayak (n)

car (n)

cycle (v)

drive (car) (v)

fly (v)

foot (n)

helicopter (n)

inline skates (n)

moped (n)

motor boat (n)

motorbike (n)

mountain bike (n)
pedal boat (n)
ride (v)
sail (v)
ship (n)
skate (v)
train (n)
wagon (n)
yacht (n)

trips

journey (n)
passenger (n)
platform (n)
return (adj) (n)
single (adj) (n)
souvenir (n)
suitcase (n)
sun cream (n)
ticket (n)
ticket office (n)
time difference (n)
travel (v)
visit (v)

culture

artists and their work

act (v)
actor (n)
celebrity (n)
famous (adj)
film (n)
hero (n)

music

band (n)
classical (n)
concert (n)
disco (n)
drum (n)
festival (n)
folk (n)
gig (n)
group (n)
heavy metal (n)
hip-hop (n)
jazz (n)

music scene (n)
musical instrument (n)
novel (n)
painting (n)
performance (n)
poem (n)
pop (n)
presenter (n)
punk (n)
rock (n)
singer (n)
TV programme (n)

sport

sports equipment

helmet (n)
knee pads (n)
rope (n)
skateboard (n)
surfboard (n)
wetsuit (n)

types of sports

athlete (n)
badminton (n)
baseball (n)
basketball (n)
competition (n)
competitor (n)
danger (n)
dangerous (adj)
dive (v)
equipment (n)
exercise (n)
fishing (n)
fit (adj)
football (n)
golf (n)
gymnastics (n)
judo (n)
karate (n)
marathon (n)
racing (n)
ride a horse (v)
rock climbing (n)
rowing (n)
rugby (n)

running (n)
skateboarding (n)
skiing (n)
sport (n)
surfing (n)
swimming (n)
tennis (n)
volleyball (n)
warm up (v)

health

illness

aspirin (n)
backache (n)
cold (n)
cough (n)
cream (n)
die (v)
disabled (adj)
doctor (n)
earache (n)
feel sick (v)
headache (n)
health (n)
hurt (v)
illness (n)
medicine (n)
overdo (v)
pain (n)
prescription (n)
sore leg (n)
sore throat (n)
stomachache (n)
take some medicine (v)
unhealthy (adj)

parts of the body

ankle (n)
arms (n)
back (n)
body (n)
cheek (of face) (n)
elbow (n)
fingers (n)
foot (n)
hands (n)
head (n)

knee (n)
leg (n)
neck (n)
shoulder (n)
stomach (n)
toes (n)

science and technology

inventions
alarm clock (n)
battery (n)
change (v)
communicate (v)
convenient (adj)
cooker (n)
easy to use (adj)
electric kettle (n)
electric toothbrush (n)
hairdryer (n)
invention (n)
magnifying glass (n)
mobile phone (n)
mobile phone charger (n)
MP3 player (n)
radio (n)
the way we live (adj)
toaster (n)
TV (n)
useful (adj)

scientific discoveries
antibiotics (n)
build (v)
design (v)
develop (v)
discover (v)
electricity (n)
experiment (v)
invent (v)
nuclear power (n)

using technology
blog (n)
chat with friends (v)
chatroom (n)

computer mouse (n)
create web pages (v)
do research (v)
download (v)
email (n)
icon (n)
instant message (v)
log on (v)
mouse mat (n)
online (adj)
password (n)
post (v)
read blogs (v)
search engines (n)
social networking sites (n)
surf (the net) (v)
text message (n)
turn off (v)
username (n)
website (n)
World Wide Web (n)

the environment

animals
crocodile (n)
goldfish (n)
monkey (n)
pig (n)
whale (n)

environmental issues
bottle (n)
cycle lane (n)
destroy (v)
dirty buildings (adj)
ecological (adj)
flood (n)
glass (n)
global warming (n)
graffiti (n)
green (cf environment) (adj)
green space (n)
lights (domestic) (n)
litter (n)
litter bin (n)

noise (n)
packaging (n)
planet (n)
plastic (n)
pollution (n)
public transport (n)
recycle (v)
recycled (adj)
rubbish (n)
save the world (v)
solar power (n)
solution (n)
tin (n)
traffic (n)
traffic-free zone (n)
western (hemisphere) (adj)
wind power (n)

landscape
canal (n)
countryside (n)
crop (n)
field (n)
mountain (n)
nature (n)
plant (n)
sea (n)
wild (adj)

natural disasters
disaster (n)
drought (n)
hurricane (n)
inhabited (adj)
rainforest (n)

weather
cloudy (adj)
cold (adj)
cool (adj)
foggy (adj)
hot (adj)
rainy (adj)
snowy (adj)
stormy (adj)
sunny (adj)
temperature (n)
warm (adj)
windy (adj)

country and society

cultural habits

blow your nose (v)
bow (v)
disability (n)
kiss (v)
make a speech (v)
member (n)
multicultural (adj)
native (adj)
offer/receive a gift (v)
population (n)
respect (n)
tax (n)
village (n)
volunteer (n)

politics

bullying (n)
crime (n)
elect (v)
election (n)
government (n)
homeless (adj)
knife crime (n)
parliament (n)
politician (n)
protest (v)
speech (n)
vote (v)
voter (n)
youth (n)

information about English-speaking countries

Alton Towers (n)
Auld Lang Syne (n)
Ben Nevis (n)
Brighton (n)
Brighton Pier (n)
Canary Wharf Tower (n)
Canberra (n)
castle (n)
City farm (n)
Everton FC (n)
fish and chips (n)
Glastonbury festival (n)
Global Cool (n)
goth (n)
Halloween party (n)
Heathrow Airport (n)
indie kid (n)
Live 8 (n)
Live Earth (n)
Liverpool (n)
Liverpool FC (n)
Manchester (n)
Manchester United (n)
Maori village (n)
Moby Dick (n)
Oxford University (n)
pound (n)
punk (n)

roller coaster (n)
Shakespeare (n)
Special Olympics (n)
St Patrick's Day (n)
Stratford-upon-Avon (n)
Sydney (n)
Sydney Opera House (n)
Tate Liverpool (n)
the Beatles Story Museum (n)
the British Museum (n)
the River Mersey (n)
the River Severn (n)
the River Thames (n)
the Science Museum (n)
Urbis Museum (n)
V Festival (n)
Windsor Castle (n)

functions list

Meeting, greeting and getting to know people

Meeting and greeting
Hello!
Hi!
This is my wife, Louise.
I'm George.
Pleased to meet you.
Bye.
Goodbye.

Getting to know people
Where are you from (in Poland)?
Have you got brothers and sisters?
How old is he?/How old are you?
Is this your first time in the UK?
What's your favourite football team?

Talking about a town

Is your town or city big or small?
Is it famous?
Are the shops good?
Are the restaurants good?
Is there a good bus or train service?
Are there any interesting museums?
Are there any parks?
What can you do in the evening?

Directions

Asking for directions
Excuse me. How do I get to the Urbis Museum?

Is the Urbis Museum near here?
Can you say that again, please?
Thank you very much.

Giving directions
Turn left into Market Street.
Then take the second right into Cross Street.
Go down Thomas Street.
Go straight on.
Urbis is on the left.
You can't miss it!

Talking about sports

What are your favourite sports?
What's your favourite football team?
Who is your favourite sports personality?
Do you do any sports?
What sports don't you like?
What sports do you watch on TV?

Expressing opinions

Giving opinions
I think it's A.
I'm sure it's B.
I think it's (antibiotics).
In my opinion (it's the TV.)
It's important because …

Responding
I agree.
I don't agree.
I'm not sure.
I don't know.

At the café

Asking the price
How much is a sandwich?
How much is it?

Saying prices
10p   ten 'p'
50p   fifty 'p'
£1.00   one pound
£5.00   five pounds
£2.50   two pounds fifty

Offering
Can I help you?
What would you like?
Anything else?

Ordering
I'll have a hot chocolate, please.
Can I have a piece of carrot cake?
I'd like a cheese and tomato sandwich, please.
A fruit juice, please.

Paying
That's £13.20, please
Here you are.
Here's your change.

Talking about food

It's healthy.
It's unhealthy.
Fruit is good for you.
Crisps aren't good for you.
Crisps are bad for you.
It's junk food.
I can't live without coffee!
I prefer juice.

Making suggestions

Making suggestions
Do you want to go to the cinema?
Come and join me.
How/What about coming with us?
Why don't you come with us?

Responding
Sure.
OK, thanks.
That's a nice/good/great idea!
I'm sorry, I can't. (I'm shopping.)

Describing a picture

In the picture I can see a kitchen/living room.
In the centre/background there is a girl.
On the right/left there's a school book.
In the background/foreground, there's a woman.
I think she is doing homework/housework.
I'm sure she's the girl's mother.

Talking about a festival

Last year, I went to (a St Patrick's Day parade.)
We watched (a big parade/fireworks.)
They ate (traditional/special food.)
She wore (traditional clothes.)
We listened to (traditional music.)

Buying tickets

Buying tickets
Can I have two tickets to Manchester Piccadilly, please?
Can I have two singles/returns to the Cornerhouse, please?
How much is a single/return ticket?
How much are they?
Is there a student reduction?

Asking for information
What platform is the next train?
Does this train go to Manchester?

Asking about a day out

Where did you go?
Who did you go with?
How did you get there?
What did you do there?
Did you enjoy it?
Where did you have lunch?

Talking about the order of activities
First …/Next …/Then …/Finally

Opinions about inventions

It's so easy to communicate now.
It changed the way we live.
It's really convenient.
It's really useful.
We use it to buy things, to watch TV …
People can travel easily.
It's easy to use.

Buying things

The shop assistant says:
Can I help you?
What size are you?
Here you are.

The customer says:
We're just looking, thanks.
I'm looking for a pair of wellies.
How much is it/are they?
Have you got a bigger size?
Can I try them on?
These are a bit small.
I'll take these, please.

Talking about holidays

Where did you go on your last holiday?
Who did you go with?
What type of holiday was it?
Where did you stay?
What did you do?
What was the best bit?
What was the worst bit?

A job interview

Where are you from?
What (other) languages do you speak?
What is your best subject at school?
Have you got any (sales) experience?
What skills and qualities have you got?
Why do you want this job?
Have you got any questions?

answer key: self-assessment tests and exam tests

self-assessment test 1

1 2 grandfather, 3 women, 4 short, 5 fair hair

2 2 packet, 3 beard, 4 card, 5 wallet

3 2 to music, 3 uniform, 4 school, 5 school, 6 lunch

4 2 watches, 3 haven't got, 4 wake up, 5 doesn't help, 6 don't cycle, 7 has got

5 2 b, 3 a, 4 c, 5 c, 6 b, 7 a

6 2 does she hang out – b,
3 do they have – e,
4 does Robert visit – f,
5 do your friends play – c,
6 do you read – a

7 1 Nick, 2 Alice, 3 Alice, 4 Tim, 5 Hannah, 6 Nick, 7 Tim, 8 Hannah

8 1 ✗, 2 ✓, 3 ✗, 4 ✗, 5 ✓, 6 ✓, 7 ✓

9 2 This – d, 3 old – b, 4 time – f, 5 Where – a, 6 favourite – c

self-assessment test 2

1 2 b, 3 a, 4 b, 5 c, 6 c, 7 a, 8 c, 9 b

2 2 sore, 3 pool, 4 stationery, 5 hospital, 6 toes, 7 flat, 8 go

3 3 ✓, 4 Do you eat many apples?
5 I haven't got any/much space on my desk.
6 Are there any sports centres in your town?
7 ✓

4 2 can't, 3 can play, 4 can do, 5 Can he, 6 Can

5 2 slowly, 3 Find, 4 good, 5 Don't watch, 6 quickly

6 1 b, 2 b, 3 c, 4 a, 5 c

7 2 Do you do any sports?
3 Is your city famous?
4 Are the shops good in your town?
5 What are your favourite sports?

8 2 get, 3 turn, 4 take, 5 can't, 6 Thank

9 1 ✓, 2 ✗, 3 ✓, 4 ✓, 5 ✗, 6 ✗

self-assessment test 3

1 2 juice, 3 meat, 4 rice, 5 bread, 6 apples, 7 tomato

2 2 hoodie, 3 skirt, 4 hat, 5 earring, 6 boots

3 2 Are you writing a letter?
3 We're/are studying history today.
4 I'm not/am not watching this film.
5 What's/is he doing?
6 Two students aren't/are not listening to the teacher.
7 Where are Tom and Robbie going?

4 2 b, 3 c, 4 b, 5 a, 6 a, 7 c

5 2 visiting, 3 'm/am doing, 4 has, 5 are wearing, 6 goes, 7 speak, 8 walking

6 1 ✓, 2 ✗, 3 ✓, 4 ✗

7 1 d, 2 b, 3 a, 4 e, 5 c

8 a 7, b 1, c 3, d 2, e 9, f 4, g 6, h 8, i 5

9 2 don't, 3 agree, 4 want

10 2 see, 3 On, 4 In

self-assessment test 4

1 2 rock, 3 folk, 4 punk, 5 hip-hop, 6 disco, 7 classical

2 2 d, 3 a, 4 e, 5 c, 6 b

3 2 way, 3 fireworks, 4 party, 5 candles, 6 parade, 7 hairdryer

4 2 went, 3 was, 4 didn't/did not finish, 5 Did you wear, 6 made, 7 weren't/were not, 8 gave, 9 Did they talk

5 1 Where did you see them?
2 When did your grandparents sell their house?
3 Who created Google?
4 How many books did you read last month?
5 Who did you talk to after the lesson?

6 1 M, 2 D, 3 P, 4 D, 5 P

7 1 b, 2 c, 3 b, 4 a, 5 b

8 2 return, 3 reduction, 4 each, 5 train

9 2 How did you get there?
3 Who did you go with?
4 What did you do there?
5 Did you enjoy it?

10 2 'm not, 3 agree

self-assessment test 5

1 2 b, 3 a, 4 a, 5 c, 6 b

2 2 c, 3 e, 4 a, 5 g, 6 d, 7 b

3 2 rubbish, 3 beach, 4 Pollution, 5 storms, 6 environment

4 2 the best, 3 more intelligent, 4 the nicest, 5 taller, 6 prettier, 7 the most beautiful, 8 the worst

5 2 am/'m not going to take, 3 is/'s going to see, 4 Are you going to help, 5 are/'re going to study

6 2 will do, 3 will not/won't be, 4 will travel

7 1 b, 2 c, 3 a, 4 b, 5 c

8 1 ✗, 2 ✗, 3 ✓, 4 ✗, 5 ✓

9 2 looking for, 3 size, 4 are, 5 try, 6 are they

10 2 good/great, 3 don't, 4 can't, 5 What, 6 thanks

self-assessment test 6

1 2 vet, 3 clerk, 4 nurse, 5 photographer, 6 assistant

2 2 polite, 3 bored, 4 reliable, 5 angry, 6 patient

3 2 have never met,
3 Have they ever voted,
4 have never made,
5 Has Barbara ever received,
6 Have you ever organised,
7 has never driven

4 2 Tom is bad at remembering names but at the same time he remembers faces very well.
3 Bethany was born on 12 March.
4 Robert is going to meet Charlie at the cinema.
5 Last Sunday I got up at eleven o'clock.

6 Eating healthy food is good for you so I'm going to some healthy food on Saturday.

5 2 Does your father have to work, 3 don't have to go, 4 has to do, 5 Do you have to be, 6 doesn't have to tidy

6 2 If you are bored, watch this programme.
3 If you want to relax, take a long bath.
4 If you feel tired, go to bed early.
5 If you go to Joe's birthday party, don't forget the present.

7 1 b, 2 a, 3 c, 4 c, 5 a

8 1 Paul, 2 Hannah, 3 Alicia, 4 Hannah, 5 Alicia, 6 Paul, 7 Alicia, 8 Paul

9 2 Where are you from?
3 What (other) languages do you speak?
4 What are your best subjects at school?
5 Have you got any teaching experience (in this kind of job)? / Have you got any experience in this kind of job? / Have you got any experience of working with children?
6 What (skills and) qualities have you got?
7 Why do you want this job?
8 Have you got any questions?

exam test 1

1 1 ✓, 2 ✗, 3 ✓, 4 ✗, 5 ✗, 6 ✓

2 1 c, 2 b, 3 c, 4 a

3 2 There, 3 plays, 4 goes, 5 to, 6 out, 7 their, 8 go, 9 watches, 10 does, 11 usually

exam test 2

1 1 b, 2 b, 3 a, 4 c, 5 c

2 1 ✗, 2 ✓, 3 ✗, 4 ✗, 5 ✓

3 1 What did Nicola Tesla invent?
2 I am mixing the salad.
3 What is your favourite food?
4 She is not wearing a hat.
5 Where did he go after the party?
6 The Internet changed the way we live.
7 Did you meet many new people at the festival?
8 I don't enjoy sleeping in a tent.
9 Can I have a return ticket to Manchester?
10 How did you celebrate the New Year?

exam test 3

1 1 e, 2 f, 3 b, 4 c, 5 a

2 1 11.00/11 o'clock/eleven o'clock, 2 sightseeing, 3 campsite, 4 beach, 5 44 795 223 098

3 2 c, 3 b, 4 b, 5 a, 6 c, 7 b, 8 a, 9 a, 10 c, 11 b

120